C000089524

1 MONTH OF
FREE
READING

at

www.ForgottenBooks.com

By purchasing this book you are eligible for one month membership to ForgottenBooks.com, giving you unlimited access to our entire collection of over 1,000,000 titles via our web site and mobile apps.

To claim your free month visit:

www.forgottenbooks.com/free907684

* Offer is valid for 45 days from date of purchase. Terms and conditions apply.

ISBN 978-0-266-90586-8
PIBN 10907684

This book is a reproduction of an important historical work. Forgotten Books uses
state-of-the-art technology to digitally reconstruct the work, preserving the original format
whilst repairing imperfections present in the aged copy. In rare cases, an imperfection in
the original, such as a blemish or missing page, may be replicated in our edition. We do,
however, repair the vast majority of imperfections successfully; any imperfections that
remain are intentionally left to preserve the state of such historical works.

Forgotten Books is a registered trademark of FB &c Ltd.
Copyright © 2018 FB &c Ltd.
FB &c Ltd, Dalton House, 60 Windsor Avenue, London, SW19 2RR.
Company number 08720141. Registered in England and Wales.

For support please visit www.forgottenbooks.com

SALE NUMBER 4431
PUBLIC EXHIBITION FROM SATURDAY, JANUARY TWENTY-EIGHTH
[WEEKDAYS 9-6 · SUNDAY 2-5]

American and English Furniture
and Decorations

PAINTINGS · PORCELAINS · HOOKED RUGS

Property of

MRS EDITH L. WILLIAMS

COHASSET, MASS.

IMPORTANT TAPESTRIES

Property of

MRS ARTHUR LIPPER

NEW YORK CITY

Property of

LEONARD M. STARBUCK

SCARSDALE, NEW YORK

Transcaspian Rugs

Further Selections from the Oriental Rug Collection of

CHARLES CALMER HART

FORMER UNITED STATES MINISTER TO PERSIA

WITH OTHER PROPERTIES
SOLD BY ORDER OF THE
VARIOUS OWNERS

Public Sale by Auction
Friday & Saturday, February 3 & 4, at 2 p. m.

AMERICAN ART ASSOCIATION
ANDERSON GALLERIES · INC

[MILTON B. LOGAN, PRESIDENT]

30 EAST 57TH STREET · NEW YORK

1939

ORDER OF SALE

---- ☆ ----

PRINTED IN U.S.A.

CONDITIONS OF SALE

The property listed in this catalogue will be offered and sold subject to the following terms and conditions:

1. The word "Company", wherever used in these Conditions of Sale, means the American Art Association-Anderson Galleries, Inc.

2. The Company has exercised reasonable care to catalogue and describe correctly the property to be sold, but it does not warrant the correctness of description, genuineness, authenticity or condition of said property.

3. All bids are to be PER LOT as numbered in the catalogue, unless otherwise announced by the auctioneer at the time of sale.

4. The highest bidder accepted by the auctioneer shall be the buyer. In the event of any dispute between bidders, the auctioneer may, in his discretion, determine who is the successful bidder, and his decision shall be final; or the auctioneer may reoffer and resell the article in dispute.

5. Any bid which is not commensurate with the value of the article offered, or which is merely a nominal or fractional advance over the previous bid, may be rejected by the auctioneer, in his discretion, if in his judgment such bid would be likely to affect the sale injuriously.

6. The name and address of the buyer of each article, or lot, shall be given to the Company immediately following the sale thereof, and payment of the whole purchase price, or such part thereof as the Company may require, shall be immediately made by the purchaser thereof. If the foregoing condition, or any other applicable condition herein, is not complied with, the sale may, at the option of the Company, be cancelled, and the article, or lot, reoffered for sale.

7. Unless the sale is advertised and announced as an unrestricted sale, or a sale without reserve, consignors reserve the right to bid.

8. Except as herein otherwise provided, title will pass to the highest bidder upon the fall of the auctioneer's hammer, and thereafter the property is at the purchaser's sole risk and responsibility.

9. Articles sold and not paid for in full and not taken by noon of the day following the sale may be turned over by the Company to a carrier to be delivered to a storehouse for the account and risk of the purchaser, and at his cost. If the purchase price has not been so paid in full, the Company may either cancel the sale,

and any partial payment already made shall thereupon be forfeited as liquidated damages, or it may resell the same, without notice to the buyer and for his account and risk, and hold him responsible for any deficiency.

10. If for any cause whatsoever any article sold cannot be delivered, or cannot be delivered in as good condition as the same may have been at the time of sale, the sale will be cancelled, and any amount that may have been paid on account of the sale will be returned to the purchaser.

11. In addition to the purchase price, the buyer will be required to pay the New York City sales tax, unless the buyer is exempt from the payment thereof.

12. The Company, subject to these Conditions of Sale and to such terms and conditions as it may prescribe, but without charge for its services, will undertake to make bids for responsible parties approved by it. Requests for such bidding must be given with such clearness as to leave no-room for misunderstanding as to the amount to be bid and must state the catalogue number of the item and the name or title of the article to be bid on. The Company reserves the right to decline to undertake to make such bids.

13. The Company will facilitate the employment of carriers and packers by purchasers but will not be responsible for the acts of such carriers or packers in any respect whatsoever.

14. These Conditions of Sale cannot be altered except in writing by the Company or by public announcement by the auctioneer at the time of sale.

SALES CONDUCTED BY A. N. BADE AND E. HAROLD L. THOMPSON

AMERICAN ART ASSOCIATION
ANDERSON GALLERIES · INC
30 EAST 57TH STREET · NEW YORK

Telephone PLAZA 3-1269   *Cable* ARTGAL *or* ANDAUCTION

MILTON B. LOGAN · *President*   JOHN T. GEERY · *Secretary and Treasurer*

FIRST SESSION

Friday, February 3, 1939, at 2 p. m.

NUMBERS 1 TO 208 INCLUSIVE

— ☆ —

DECORATIVE AND TABLE GLASS
AND PORCELAIN

1. CUT GLASS DECANTER AND TWELVE HOLLOW-STEM WINE GLASSES
   With ten paneled glass trays. Together 23 pieces.

2. COLLECTION OF GLASS VASES AND CANDLESTICKS
   Comprising gold-decorated rose-colored two-handled vase with cover, green diamond-diapered vase, pink Nailsea glass candlestick, tall silvered glass candlestick, and cut clear glass candlestick. Together 5 pieces.
   Heights, 7½ to 14 inches

3. BRISTOL THREE-PIECE PINK GLASS GARNITURE
   Comprising two bottles, with gilded stoppers, and a vase. Accompanied by two sapphire blue perfume bottles enriched with gold tracery. Together 5 pieces.
   Heights, 5⅞ to 8¼ inches

4. COLLECTION OF FIVE BLOWN AND PRESSED GLASS OBJECTS
   Comprising a large aquamarine jar, an apple green bottle, a clear glass leaf-decorated bottle, a double-ringed decanter with heart-shaped stopper, and a covered glass jar.
   Heights, 8 to 13½ inches

5. ELEVEN FLOWER-CUT CHAMPAGNE GLASSES AND
   ELEVEN DIAMOND-CUT WINE GLASSES
   With six gold-decorated finger bowls having trays. Together 34 pieces.

6. NEW ENGLAND THREE-MOLD CLEAR GLASS BRANDY DECANTER
   Of flattened globular form with handle and lipped neck; decorated in loop design; teardrop stopper. Rare.
   Height, 8½ inches

7. NEW ENGLAND THREE-MOLD CLEAR GLASS DECANTER
   With globular stopper, triple-ringed neck. Decorated with diamond diaper and vertical ribbing.
   Height, 10½ inches

8. NEW ENGLAND CLEAR GLASS LARGE JAR
   Of cylindrical form, with folded rim. Rare.
   Height, 10½ inches; diameter, 12 inches

9. NEW ENGLAND MOLDED AND ETCHED GLASS PITCHER
   AND FOUR TUMBLERS
   Engraved with berry and leaf spray and ornamented with applied rosettes. Accompanied by a Sheffield plate cruet stand containing four New England three-mold clear glass condiment bottles. Together 6 pieces.

10. COLLECTION OF PRESSED CLEAR GLASS TABLE OBJECTS
Comprising two covered compotes, fruit dish on stand, and circular deep dish, all in sawtooth pattern; also a square berry dish in geometric pattern. Together 5 pieces.

11. BLOWN AND ETCHED CLEAR GLASS DECANTER
AND FIVE WINE GLASSES
Engraved in grapevine pattern. Decanter with vertically ribbed base, triple-ringed neck, and flat stopper.

12. TWELVE BLOWN CLEAR GLASS SPORTING GOBLETS
Intaglio cut with fox-hunting scene.

13. COLLECTION OF PRESSED CLEAR GLASS TABLE OBJECTS
Comprising a plateau in sawtooth pattern, two deep dishes in diamond waffle design, two relish dishes in the shape of fish, and two butter dishes with cow medallion and serrated edge. Together 7 pieces.

14. TWO STAFFORDSHIRE GROUPS
Youth and maiden, and children robbing birds' nests.
Heights, 11½ and 12 inches

15. TWO MEISSEN PORCELAIN STATUETTES
Figure of a youth in flowered garments, leaning on garden implements; and a figure of a winged beggar boy. *Heights, 7¼ and 8½ inches*

16. SÈVRES PORCELAIN CHOCOLATE SERVICE
Comprising chocolate pot, sugar bowl, and creamer. Decorated with painted scenes in the style of Watteau. Accompanied by eight Haviland Limoges china teacups, eleven saucers, and two cake plates; decorated with dainty floral borders. Together 24 pieces.

17. COLLECTION OF PORCELAIN TABLE OBJECTS
Comprising three divided supper dishes, two of which have lobster handles, fruit dish, cake plate, game plate, and deep dish. Together 7 pieces.

18. FLOWER-DECORATED LIMOGES PORCELAIN BREAKFAST SERVICE
Comprising teapot, covered sugar bowl, creamer, two cups and saucers, and one plate. Accompanied by six Limoges dessert plates with garland border, and five cabinet ornaments. Together 19 pieces.

19. ORIENTAL PORCELAIN PART DESSERT SERVICE
Comprising two oval platters and six plates; decorated in variations of the Imari pattern. *Diameters, 8 to 12 inches*

[See illustration of part on page 14]

20. WORCESTER PORCELAIN ALE SET
Comprising tray holding jug and three mugs decorated in red and white chintz pattern. Accompanied by six Limoges flower-decorated dessert plates, nine French porcelain after-dinner coffee cups and saucers, a chocolate pot, six teacups and saucers, and two cake plates; variously decorated. Some slightly chipped. Together 43 pieces.

21. GOLD-DECORATED AND PAINTED PORCELAIN FISH SET
Comprising fish platter and eleven plates, having centres painted with scene of trout rising from water. Accompanied by eight square oyster plates, one chipped. Together 20 pieces.
Length of platter, 23¼ inches; diameter of plates, 8¾ inches; oyster plates, 7¾ inches square

22. COLLECTION OF ORIENTAL BLUE AND WHITE TABLE PORCELAIN
Comprising eight covered bowls, fan-shaped dish, nine fish-shaped sauce dishes, circular deep dish, six after-dinner coffee cups and saucers, cake plate, three small bowls, and tea caddy; a few chipped. Together 36 pieces.

23. COLLECTION OF ORIENTAL TABLE PORCELAIN
Comprising one large scalloped plate, three bowls, and six plates; decorated in several versions of the Imari pattern. Together 10 pieces.
Diameters, 5¾ to 12 inches

24. TWO IMARI PORCELAIN BOWLS
Large bowls; one scalloped, the other with flaring rim. Richly decorated in panels enclosing fish and floral forms in five colors.
Diameters, 12 and 10 inches

25. SET OF SIX PURPLE LUSTRE DECORATED STAFFORDSHIRE POTTERY CUPS AND SAUCERS
With purple lustre borders enclosing printed medallion temperance emblem. Accompanied by two transfer-decorated plates in red and green, and chocolate pot and tea caddy with fluted bodies decorated in the Worcester manner in the Chinese taste; the tea caddy with metal cover. Together 16 pieces.

[See illustration of part on page 14]

26. COLLECTION OF PEWTER AND GLASS OBJECTS
Comprising pewter eggcup holder containing four porcelain cups, three clear glass spirit lamps, miniature etched glass vase, turquoise blue covered dish with lamb finial, paperweight, and salt shaker. Together 8 pieces.

27. PAIR ROBIN'S-EGG BLUE GLASS LUSTRES
In the Victorian taste. Scalloped bowl painted with birds and gilded scrolls; baluster shaft and spreading feet. Crystal prisms.
Height, 13 inches

28. TWO STAFFORDSHIRE POTTERY COTTAGE ORNAMENTS
The Highland Lovers; and *The Harvesters.*
Heights, 13¾ and 12½ inches

29. JAPANESE PORCELAIN MANTEL GARNITURE
Comprising a covered jar and two vases. Decorated in iron red enclosing reserves of peony and bird forms. Accompanied by two covered vases enriched with aubergine and green floral decoration on a light green ground. Repaired. Together 5 pieces. *Heights, 7½ and 9½ inches*

30. COLLECTION OF FOUR ORIENTAL PORCELAIN DECORATIVE OBJECTS
Comprising square covered box in blue and white hawthorn pattern,
slender vase with petunia-shaped top, covered jar decorated in blue, and
large teapot with wicker handle and figural scenes in colored enamels.

31. PAIR BOHEMIAN MILK WHITE GLASS LUSTRES
Decorated with gold tracery and hung with cut crystal glass pendants.
Accompanied by three opalescent glass lamp shades. Together 5 pieces.
Height of lustres, 15 inches

32. CAPO DI MONTE PORCELAIN EWER
Large urn-shaped vessel embellished with a frieze of figure and animal
subjects in soft pastel shades; sloping shoulder, gilded voluted neck;
satyr- and figure-scrolled handle. *Height, 20 inches*

DECORATIVE OIL PAINTINGS AND PRINTS

33. EARLY MAP OF NEW YORK STATE
Engraved by Simeon De Witt; published in 1804. Large folio, framed.

34. PORTRAIT OF A GENTLEMAN *American, Early XIX Century*
Primitive portrait on pine panel, removed from an overmantel in a house
in Hadley, Massachusetts. *Height, 30½ inches; width, 23 inches*

35. WASHINGTON'S FIRST INTERVIEW WITH HIS WIFE *Engraved by Hall*
Line engraving after Ehringer. Published N. Y. and Boston, 1863.
Walnut frame.

36. TWO COLOR PRINTS
Lafayette and The Declaration of Independence of the United States of
America; framed.

37. FOUR SILHOUETTES WITH AUTOGRAPHS *After Brown*
Thomas Hart Benton, franked *"Thomas H. Benton"*; Richard Menton
Johnson, franked *"Rh M. Johnson"*; De Witt Clinton, document signed;
Daniel Webster, document signed.

38. FOUR SILHOUETTES WITH AUTOGRAPHS *After Brown*
Andrew Jackson, document signed as President; John Forsyth, document
signed as Secretary of State; Levi Woodbury, franked signature; John
Caldwell Calhoun, signed *"J. C. Calhoun"*.

39. PORTRAIT OF LINCOLN: MEZZOTINT *By Sartain, after E. D. Marchant*
Published in 1864. Accompanied by a tinted lithograph, 'The New Era
of the American Nation' commemorating the signing of the Thirteenth
Amendment. Lithograph by Bufford, framed. Together 2 pieces.

40. TERRA COTTA MEDALLION OF BENJAMIN FRANKLIN
Circular bust portrait in *bas relief* of Benjamin Franklin in profile to the
left; with peripheral inscription, *Eripuit Coelo Fulmen, Sceptrumque
Tirannis;* signed B. NINI F 1779. Framed. *Diameter, 5 inches*

41. TERRA COTTA MEDALLION OF BENJAMIN FRANKLIN
Circular medallion showing *bas-relief* bust portrait of Benjamin Franklin in profile facing *left*; with peripheral inscription; signed NINI F 1777. Framed. *Framed. 3¾ inches*

42. HAND-COLORED MID-VICTORIAN PRINT
Representing a mother at the bedside of her *sleeping* child.
Height, 23¾ inches; width, 17¾ inches

43. THE FALL OF MAN: EARLY WOODCUT *Probably Pennsylvania Dutch*
Quaintly colored woodcut in carved wood frame.

44. MEZZOTINT ENGRAVING PRINTED IN COLORS
E. F. Hubbard, Contemporary English
'Mona Lisa'. Accompanied by 'Portrait of a Young Country Girl', color reproduction, framed. Together 2 pieces.

45. TWO AMERICAN CHROMOLITHOGRAPHS
'The *Well* Sweep' and 'Mother and Children'. Both about 1860. Framed.

46. THREE STIPPLE ENGRAVINGS PRINTED IN COLORS
'Telling Fortunes', by P. Marcuard *after* J. Northcote, in gilded frame; two mythological subjects in *black* glass mats, framed.

47. TWO STIPPLE ENGRAVINGS PRINTED IN CARMINE
F. Bartolozzi, Italian: 1725-1815
'A St. James Beauty'; 'A St. Giles Beauty'. Accompanied by silhouette portrait, engraved portrait of Sir Thomas More, and mezzotint by Richard Earlom. Framed. Together 5 pieces.

48. FLOWER PRINTS
Collection of ten colored lithograph flower prints by D. W. Moody; framed.

49. WINTER
Colored lithograph by Haskell and Allen. Published in Boston. Large folio, framed.

50. BLACK MONDAY, OR THE DEPARTURE FOR SCHOOL; DULCE DOMUM OR THE RETURN FROM SCHOOL. *Pair in colors after Bigg.*
Reproductions of the rare mezzotints engraved by John Jones. Framed.

51. THE RETREAT FROM LEIPSIG; YORK MINSTER. *Two large etchings.*
Both signed proofs. The first by Jules Jacquet after Meissonier; the second by Charles Bird. Framed.

52. ETCHING *Samuel Colman, N.A., American: 1832-1920*
'Olive Trees of the Riviera'; good impression, framed.
Height, 10½ inches; length, 14 inches

53. 'FLORA MCIVOR': RACEHORSE
Fine pastel drawing of a famous running horse; Dated 1861, signed
W E W. Framed.   *Height, 20½ inches; length, 29 inches*

54. TWO RACE HORSE PORTRAITS: PAIR MEZZOTINTS
By Brookshaw, after Sartorious and Shaw
'Eclipse' and 'Brilliant'. Published, London, 1770. In contemporary
frames.

On the back of one is an interesting account of the history of these prints,
which originally belonged to the groom and veterinary to King
George III of England

55. THREE ENGLISH SPORTING PRINTS: COLORED AQUATINTS
'Alice Hawthorne', 'The Team', and 'The Hunting Stud'; engraved by
Hunt and Harris, all after Herring, 1844-1846. All framed.

56. COACHING PRINT IN COLORS   *By J. Harris, after C. C. Henderson*
'Changing Horses', Fores's Coaching Recollections. Published by Messrs.
Fores, London, 1842. Large folio,-framed.

57. TWO OIL PAINTINGS
Landscape ascribed to Blakelock, and Belgian town scene on panel.
Height, 12 inches; width, 5¾ inches
Height, 7½ inches; width, 5¾ inches

58. SCENE ON THE HUDSON RIVER   *Signed, E. Boudin*
Oil painting. Hill at left, cottages and landing place at right.
Height, 14 inches; length, 24 inches

59. OIL PAINTING   *Flemish, Late XVI Century*
'Conversion of St. Paul'; on copper. Accompanied by a sanguine drawing
of the Magdalen. Together 2 pieces.
Height of painting, 10½ inches; length, 15 inches
Height of drawing, 8¾ inches; width, 5¾ inches

60. ITALIAN LANDSCAPE   *Attributed to Zuccarelli*
Oil painting. Countryside with a stream, house, and barn as well as ruins
animated by figures and a pair of oxen.
Height, 17½ inches; length, 23¼ inches

61. TWO OIL PAINTINGS
'The Smoker', in the manner of Teniers; 'The Alchemist', attributed to
Charles Muller. Both on panels. *Height, 9½ inches; width, 7½ inches*
Height, 7 inches; width, 5 inches

62. CLEOPATRA WITH THE ASP   *Italian, XVII Century*
Oil painting. Depicted at-half length, seated, in robe and light tan turban.
Height, 40½ inches; width, 36½ inches

63. BUST PORTRAIT OF GEORGE WASHINGTON   *C. Alexander*

Oil painting. Signed at the *lower left* and inscribed *After Stuart.*

Academy board: Height, 10¾ *inches; width,* 8¾ *inches*

64. OIL PAINTING

Portrait study of an urchin.   *Height,* 18 *inches; width,* 15 *inches*

65. AN ANGEL   *Attributed to Guido Reni*

Oil painting. Depicted at nearly half *length* in green *robe* with gold embroidery, holding a stalk of lilies. Painted within an oval spandrel.

Height, 29 *inches; width,* 23 *inches*

66. MADONNA GLORIOSA

After the Sienese Master Sano di Pietro di Menico

Oil painting. The Virgin, robed in blue and holding the *Infant* Christ with flowerpot in His hands, is flanked by two female saints in brilliant garments, holding their symbols; above in a roundel appears the image of Christ. Brilliant *sgraffito* ground with armorial bearings in spandrels. Carved and gilded tabernacle frame in the Gothic taste.

Cradled panel: Height, 18½ *inches; width,* 9¾ *inches*

AMERICAN AND ENGLISH FURNITURE
AND DECORATIONS

67. HISTORICAL PRINTED CHINTZ FRAGMENT   *Early XIX Century*

Commemorative chintz with portrait of Washington and '1776' printed in sepia in medallion placed between rose-colored shields containing scales of justice '& Peace'; in old gilded frame.

Height, 6 *inches; length,* 6⅜ *inches*

68. EAGLE-DECORATED TÔLE WARE CHANDELIER

Painted light green with eagle decoration in gold, with three candle sockets; fitted for electricity.   *Height,* 14½ *inches; diameter,* 11 *inches*

69. MARINE WOOLWORK PICTURE   *English, Early XIX Century*

Square-rigged barque with all sails set, flying the Union Jack; embroidered in crewel work. Soft gray-blue sky and blue sea. Contemporary gold frame.   *Height,* 22 *inches; length,* 27½ *inches*

'70' PINE SPICE BOX AND FRUITWOOD CANDLE BRACKET

New England, Early XIX Century

Spice box with original red paint, containing nine drawers. Bracket with sides and back finely scalloped.

Height of spice box, 8¾ *inches; length,* 12¼ *inches; height of bracket,* 15½ *inches*

71. FOUR PINE FOOTSTOOLS   *New England, XIX Century*

Two with oval tops, the others oblong.

72. SHERATON INLAID MAHOGANY SHAVING MIRROR

English, Early XIX Century

12 5⁶ Rectangular mirror with quadrangular supports over a bow-front case fitted with one drawer.   *Height, 21½ inches; width, 21½ inches*

73. OVAL DECORATED LAQUÉ TRAY ON STAND

Painted with medallions and flower forms and inlaid with mother-of-pearl on black background; on turned cross-stretchered legs.

Height, 20¼ inches; length, 29½ inches

74. CARVED MAHOGANY HANGING SHELF   *Chippendale Style*

10 - Two shelves placed between pierced ends on serpentine box containing two small drawers.   *Height, 23½ inches; width, 21 inches*

75. SHERATON MAHOGANY SIDEBOARD

Rectangular top with bowed centre section overhanging two long drawers flanked by a smaller drawer above a hinged cupboard; molded plinth base.   *Height, 36 inches; length, 5 feet 4 inches*

76. BIRCH SATIN-UPHOLSTERED ARMCHAIR   *Louis XVI Style*

17 5⁶ Oval molded back, serpentine seat, and fluted tapering legs. Upholstered in ivory satin.

77. PINE HANGING SHELF   *New England, Early XIX Century*

7 5⁶ Scrolled ends supporting three graduated scalloped shelves.

Height, 33 inches; width, 23 inches

78. EMPIRE CARVED AND GILDED ACORN WALL MIRROR

American, circa 1830

10 Upright frame with molded break-front cornice and acorn pendants, supported by turned and rope-carved split balusters.

Height, 36 inches; width, 23½ inches

79. MAPLE SEWING TABLE   *New England, Early XIX Century*

Box-shaped case with hinged top enclosing tray containing fitted compartments; frieze with one drawer; turned tapering legs. Restored.

17 5⁶   *Height, 30½ inches; width, 18½ inches*

80. CHILD'S MAPLE AND HICKORY SLAT-BACK ARMCHAIR

New England, XVIII Century

5 Two arched slats, turned arms and turned supports; rear supports with small finials. Turned box stretcher, rush seat.

81. MAHOGANY AND SATINWOOD BEDSIDE TABLE   *Sheraton Style*

Square top on outset ring-turned and reeded tapering legs; deep apron containing two shallow drawers faced with satinwood.

2 0—   *Height, 29 inches; width, 20¼ inches*

82. CARVED MAHOGANY DUMBWAITER

15 Three circular molded dish trays supported by turned and carved shaft; tripod support, claw and ball feet.   *Height, 44 inches; diameter, 24 inches*

[NUMBERS 83 AND 84]

83. CARVED MAHOGANY GALLERY-TOP TABLE   *Chippendale Style*
Rectangular top with Gothic arch and leaf scroll pierced gallery on square
legs with chamfered inside corners; pierced brackets, cross stretcher.
                              Height, 28 inches; width, 18½ inches

[See illustration]

84. CARVED MAHOGANY REVOLVING-TOP DRUM TABLE   *Sheraton Style*
Tooled and gilded red leather-covered circular top with reeded edge, containing four small cockbeaded drawers on vase-turned shaft and reeded
tripod base.   *Height, 27½ inches; diameter, 24 inches*

[See illustration]

85. SHERATON INLAID MAHOGANY WORK TABLE
Square cyma-shaped top over two drawers of conforming shape with split
ring-turned pilasters extending into slightly bulbous tapered legs.
                              Height, 28½ inches; width, 17½ inches

86. SHERATON INLAID MAHOGANY WORK TABLE
Matching the preceding.   *Height, 28½ inches; width, 17½ inches*

87. CARVED WALNUT AND BLUE-GREEN DAMASK-UPHOLSTERED SOFA
Serpentine-shaped back, outscrolled arms; base elaborately carved with
leaf and shell motives.   *Length, 6 feet 2 inches*

9

88. PAIR *INLAID* MAHOGANY HALF-ROUND CONSOLE TABLES

Hepplewhite Style

32 56 Semicircular tops crossbanded in satinwood; square tapering legs with spade feet.　　　　*Height, 28½ inches; width, 22 inches*

89. TWO BIRD'S-EYE MAPLE MIRRORS　　　*New England, XIX Century*

15 Rectangular molded frames; new plate glass mirrors.

Heights, 24 and 30 inches

90. NEW ENGLAND MAPLE TEA TABLE

40 Oblong molded top, scalloped frieze, cabriole legs ending in heart-shaped feet.　　　　*Height, 25 inches; length, 32 inches*

91. MAHOGANY AND MAPLE FIELD BEDSTEAD　　*American, XIX Century*

Single size bed with slender turned front posts and quadrangular tapered

45 backposts, shaped headboard; bell-shaped canopy. Restored.

Height, 5 feet; length, 6 feet 6 inches; width, 41 inches

92. CARVED MAHOGANY TRIPOD STAND　　　*Chippendale Style*

Dish top on fluted shaft and cabriole legs terminating in snake feet.

10 - *Height, 23 inches; diameter, 16 inches*

93. MAPLE AND PINE SLAT-BACK ARMCHAIR AND SIDE CHAIR

New England, Early XVIII Century

15 Armchair with five slats, turned arms, mushroom finials on front posts; turned supports and stretchers, rush seat. Side chair with four arched slats, turned supports and stretchers, and rush seat.

94. QUEEN ANNE WALNUT LOWBOY

30- Oblong molded top on a case containing one shallow and two deep drawers; triple-arched skirt, cabriole legs with pad feet.

Height, 29 inches; length, 30 inches

95. HEPPLEWHITE INLAID MAHOGANY OVAL-TOP PEMBROKE TABLE

Slightly bowed centre section with two semi-oval shaped drop leaves

30 crossbanded in satinwood; frieze contains one drawer; geometrically inlaid paneled tapering legs.　*Height, 29½ inches; length open, 42 inches*

96. CARVED MAHOGANY PIECRUST TRIPOD STAND　　*Chippendale Style*

Top with ribbon-carved edge on fluted shaft and acanthus-carved cabriole

10- legs terminating in claw and ball feet.

Height, 23 inches; diameter, 16 inches

97. CHIPPENDALE CARVED MAHOGANY TILT-TOP TABLE

Cyma-carved circular top on hinged bird cage on carved baluster shaft

Pan and carved tripod support.　*Height, 28½ inches; diameter, 30 inches*

98. MAHOGANY SLANT-FRONT DESK   *English, XVIII Century*
Hinged flap enclosing a fitted interior containing pigeonholes and drawers,
over four drawers of graduated depth; bracket feet. Some restoration.
Height, 41 inches; width, 38 inches

30-

99. MAPLE AND ASH LADDER-BACK ARMCHAIR AND SIDE CHAIR
                              New Hampshire, XVIII Century
Armchair with three arched slats, sloping arm rests, turned supports,
sausage-turned frontal stretcher, and rush seat; side chair somewhat
similar.

2 16

100. INLAID MAHOGANY BONNET-TOP SMALL SECRETARY
The upper part consisting of two gothic-arched doors enclosing adjustable
shelves above two small drawers and surmounted by a hooded swanneck
pediment with carved rosaces; lower part with hinged writing flap, four
long drawers, and splayed feet.
Height, 6 feet 3 inches; width, 26 inches

70-

101. INLAID MAHOGANY CHEST OF DRAWERS
In the American Hepplewhite taste; deep rich mahogany case of two short
and three long drawers, paneled with satinwood stringing.
Height, 37 inches; length, 41 inches

30-

102. MAPLE TALL-POST BEDSTEAD   *Connecticut, XVIII Century*
Slender and tapered octagonal posts with hand-wrought iron canopy
hooks.   *Height, 6 feet 10 inches*

10-

103. SHERATON INLAID MAHOGANY SECRETARY DESK
The upper part with triple gothic-arched glazed doors above two shallow
drawers; lower part with hinged writing flap and three long drawers.
Height, 6 feet 6 inches; width, 37 inches

45-

104. CURLY MAPLE SMALL SIDEBOARD   *Hepplewhite Style*
Arched centre section containing one drawer flanked by two drawers
placed between square tapering legs; oval brasses. Drawers and arch outlined in cockbeaded molding.   *Height, 36 inches; length, 5 feet*

2 -

105. HEPPLEWHITE INLAID MAHOGANY BOW-FRONT CHEST OF DRAWERS
Convex-fronted top edged with checkered inlay over a case of four long
drawers of conforming shape paneled with satinwood stringing; splayed
French feet. Lion brass bail handles.
Height, 35 inches; length, 39 inches

6 -

11

[NUMBER 106]

106. HEPPLEWHITE INLAID MAHOGANY BEAU BRUNNEL

English, circa 1785

Dressing table with boxed and hinged flap top disclosing a fitted interior banded in satinwood with covered box-like compartment and adjustable dressing mirror; paneled frieze containing a sliding tray, quadrangular tapering and inlaid legs, spade feet.

Height, 30½ *inches; width,* 22½ *inches*

[See illustration]

107. PAIR CARVED MAPLE LOW-POST BEDSTEADS

Turned and pineapple-carved posts, shaped headboards, and turned and carved foot rails. *Length,* 6 *feet* 6 *inches; width.* 40 *inches*

108. SHERATON MAHOGANY TAMBOUR SECRETARY DESK

The upper part consisting of rectangular box-shaped compartment fitted with husk and swag inlaid tambour shutter enclosing a fitted interior; lower part with hinged writing flap and two long drawers. Square tapering legs with spade feet. Painted porcelain ring handles.

Height, 45 *inches; width,* 34 *inches*

12

109. CURLY MAPLE SMALL CHEST OF DRAWERS *Massachusetts, circa 1760*
Rectangular top with molded edge on case of four graduated drawers;
molded base, bracket feet.   *Height, 31½ inches; length, 39 inches*

110. QUEEN ANNE MAHOGANY BONNET-TOP HIGHBOY
In two parts, the upper section with four long drawers below three
smaller ones, the central drawer carved with fan, surmounted by cyma-
molded broken-arch pediment; lower section consisting of one long drawer
above three small ones. Triple-arcaded skirt, cabriole legs with pad feet.
                               Height, 6 feet 8 inches; width, 37½ inches

111. GEORGIAN INLAID MAHOGANY BREAK-FRONT BOOKCASE
The upper section having one large and two small latticed glazed doors
enclosing adjustable shelves, surmounted by a crotch mahogany frieze
with dentiled cornice; lower part with slightly bowed centre section
containing three deep drawers flanked by paneled cupboards. Molded
base.   *Height, 6 feet 8 inches; width, 49 inches*

112. SET OF EIGHT HEPPLEWHITE CARVED MAHOGANY DINING CHAIRS
Comprising two armchairs and six side chairs; molded shield-shaped
backs with pierced splat carved with sheaf of wheat and husks, centring
inlaid oval satinwood paterae. Serpentine seats, molded tapered quadrangular legs with box stretcher. Seats covered in striped fabric patterned
with laurel leaf.

113. CHIPPENDALE CROTCH MAHOGANY CHEST OF DRAWERS
Small case of desirable size, with molded top and four long drawers faced
with matched crotch mahogany and cockbeaded edges; bracket feet.
                                Height, 32 inches; length, 35½ inches

114. GEORGIAN INLAID MAHOGANY SERPENTINE SIDEBOARD
Cyma-shaped top edged with satinwood over one long drawer flanked by
smaller drawers and cupboard; paneled and inlaid with satinwood crossbanding, paterae, and fans. Quadrangular tapering legs and spade feet.
                                      Height, 37 inches; length, 5 feet

115. GEORGIAN MAHOGANY AND MAPLE BREAK-FRONT
SECRETARY BOOKCASE
The recessed upper part consisting of one large compartment flanked by
smaller compartments with latticed and glazed doors enclosing adjustable
shelves; lower part of conforming shape centred by a sliding writing compartment with hinged flap above two long drawers flanked by a short
drawer over a cupboard. Ogee bracket feet. The whole profusely crossbanded and faced with maple, decorated with semicircular motives.
                                Height, 7 feet 2 inches; width, 45 inches

13

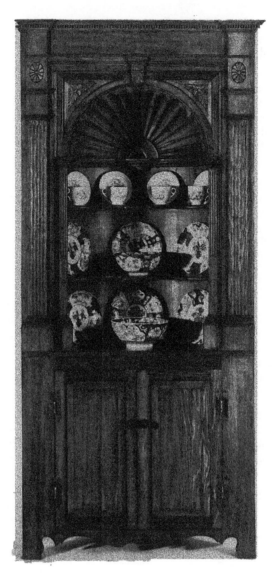

[NUMBER 116]

STAFFORDSHIRE CUPS AND SAUCERS (TOP ROW): NUMBER 25
ORIENTAL PORCELAIN PART DESSERT SERVICE (LOWER TWO ROWS): NUMBER 19

116. AMERICAN CARVED PINE CORNER CUPBOARD

60-   Triangular cabinet with carved arched recessed shell over two shaped
shelves flanked by fluted pilasters and surmounted by a dentiled cornice;
lower part fitted with two paneled doors enclosing shelf.

Height, 6 feet 8 inches; width, 35 inches

[See illustration]

117. AMERICAN CARVED PINE CORNER CUPBOARD
Matching the preceding.   *Height, 6 feet 8 inches; width, 35 inches*

6 o -

118. SHERATON INLAID MAHOGANY THREE-PART DINING TABLE
Comprising a central section with baluster shaft on quadrangular splayed
support and two end sections on tripod; the top with reeded edge and
crossbanded in satinwood. Two extra leaves.
Height, 29 inches; length extended, 11 feet 2 inches; width, 46 inches

119. COLLECTION OF THREE COPPER SHIP'S OBJECTS
Covered grog can and two ship's lights; imperfect.

120. BLUE AND WHITE POTTERY GARDEN SEAT
Barrel-shaped, decorated with allover chrysanthemum pattern in shades
of blue.   *Height, 18½ inches*

HOOKED RUGS

121. FLORAL HOOKED RUG
Multicolored blocked border enclosing a diamond medallion centring and
flanked by old-fashioned roses.
Length, 3 feet 1 inch; width, 2 feet 4 inches

122. SCROLL HOOKED RUG
Bold coral scrolls enclosing a soft tan field.
Length, 4 feet 4 inches; width, 2 feet 3 inches

123. MOTTO HOOKED RUG
Best Wishes on a warm sand ground with scrolls and naturalistic roses.
Length, 3 feet 11 inches; width, 2 feet

124. FLORAL HOOKED RUG
Small oval mat with floral sprays and bouquet worked in naturalistic
colors.   *Length, 4 feet 1 inch; width, 2 feet 1 inch*

125. GEOMETRIC HOOKED RUG
Multicolored small circles forming a diamond.
Length, 4 feet 2 inches; width, 2 feet 4 inches

126. BEDSIDE HOOKED RUG
Soft brown scrolls enclosing detached floral sprays in rose and green.
Length, 3 feet 8 inches; width, 1 foot 10 inches

127. GEOMETRIC HOOKED RUG
Large squares worked in multicolored stripes, connected at the corners
with smaller squares in reds and greens.
Length, 6 feet 11 inches; width, 5 feet 10 inches

15

[NUMBERS 128 AND 129]

128. MARINE THRESHOLD MAT

Olive ground centring fully rigged barque flanked by cornucopiae above the inscription *Welcome*. *Length, 3 feet 7 inches; width, 2 feet 6 inches*

[See illustration]

129. LOCOMOTIVE HOOKED RUG

Old-fashioned flower sprays enclosing a cartouche with locomotive and train of cars worked in shades of brown.

Length, 3 feet 9 inches; width, 2 feet

[See illustration]

130. FLORAL HOOKED RUG
Soft blue scalloped border enclosing a variegated cream and tan field centred with an oval floral medallion worked in shades of red, green, tan, and mauve. *Length, 4 feet 11 inches; width, 2 feet 5 inches*

131. GEOMETRIC HOOKED RUG
Large diamond with geometrical arrangement of multicolored smaller diamonds. *Length, 5 feet; width, 2 feet 8 inches*

132. GEOMETRIC HOOKED RUG
Ribbon design in shades of blue, tan, and rose.
Length, 6 feet; width, 2 feet 10 inches

133. FLORAL HOOKED RUG
Trailing crimson flowers enclosing a light shaped oblong panel.
Length, 4 feet 3 inches; width, 2 feet 5 inches

134. FLORAL HOOKED RUG
Amethyst border with detached floral sprigs enclosing a diamond with sand ground and similar decoration.
Length, 5 feet 1 inch; width, 4 feet 3 inches

135. BIRD HOOKED RUG
Vermilion framed cartouche enclosing a spread-winged robin perched on a leafy branch, the ends with radiating scrolled floral forms. Interesting example of raised work. *Length, 4 feet 9 inches; width, 2 feet 7 inches*

136. GEOMETRIC HOOKED RUG
Warm tan ground with variously colored pinwheels.
Length, 4 feet 3 inches; width, 2 feet 6 inches

137. PRIMITIVE HOOKED RUG
Speckled gray ground with a central panel of double heart and scrolls in shades of salmon and yellow.
Length, 5 feet 7 inches; width, 2 feet 2 inches

138. ANIMAL HOOKED RUG
The centre occupied by a horse's head within a horseshoe, surrounded by leaf sprays worked in shades of brown, tan, gray, and rose.
Length, 4 feet 1 inch; width, 2 feet 4 inches

139. GEOMETRIC HOOKED RUG
Variegated tan and green ground, the central panel with multicolored snowflakes; tile-like borders.
Length, 4 feet 4 inches; width, 2 feet 9 inches

140. THREE HOOKED RUGS
Welcome mat with blue ground and floral border, a basket-of-flowers mat, and a geometric and floral rug. Worn.

141. FLORAL HOOKED RUG

Formal arrangement of leaves and scrolls enclosing a spray of flowers in rose and green. *Length, 4 feet 3 inches; width, 2 feet 6 inches*

142. HOOKED RUNNER

Conventionalized snowflake forms in colors on a variegated black and blue field enclosed by rose scroll. *Length, 6 feet; width, 1 foot 7 inches*

143. FLORAL HOOKED RUG

Chinese pattern; warm tan oblong field with quaint flower pots at either end, the centre with a scrolled motive. Border of flower baskets and geometric forms. *Length, 5 feet; width, 2 feet 10 inches*

144. FLORAL HOOKED RUG

Variegated brown ground decorated with hollyhocks in naturalistic colors. *Length, 4 feet 6 inches; width, 2 feet 3 inches*

145. BASKET-OF-FLOWERS HOOKED RUG

Centre with basket of flowers worked in soft shades of tan, rose, and cream, the corners with scrolled American shield. *Length, 4 feet 3 inches; width, 2 feet 7 inches*

146. GEOMETRIC HOOKED RUG

Multicolored pattern of blocked motives. *Length, 5 feet 10 inches; width, 2 feet 10 inches*

147. FLORAL HOOKED RUG

Variegated tan ground centring a scrolled cartouche with floral bouquet worked in deep crimson, scarlet, and green. *Length, 5 feet 1 inch; width, 2 feet 6 inches*

148. FLORAL HOOKED RUG

Daisies and roses on a shaded green-black ground. *Length, 5 feet 1 inch; width, 2 feet 7 inches*

149. BIRD HOOKED RUG

Birds and flowers worked in canary yellow and mauve on a soft blue ground. *Length, 3 feet 1 inch; width, 2 feet 7 inches*

150. GEOMETRIC HOOKED RUG

Geometrical medallion enclosing small bouquet in red, taupe, mauve, and green on a softly shaded gray-green field; border of bouquets and sprays worked with geometrical precision. *Length, 7 feet 4 inches; width, 6 feet*

151. COOKIE HOOKED RUG

Candy-striped border enclosing a brown field with multicolored circular cookie forms. *Length, 3 feet; width, 2 feet 3 inches*

18

152. FLORAL HOOKED RUG

Various shades of tan with faded scroll surrounding a small bouquet.

Length, 4 feet 11 inches; width, 3 feet 3 inches

7 ⁵⁶

153. ANIMAL HOOKED RUG

A cat and two kittens at play on a rose-colored hearth rug.

Length, 4 feet 1 inch; width, 2 feet 6 inches

7 ⁵⁶

154. GEOMETRIC HOOKED RUG

Dove gray ground with two large multicolored serrated squares.

Length, 5 feet 11 inches; width, 3 feet

1 ⁵

155. 'WELCOME' THRESHOLD RUG

Semicircular rug with fully rigged clipper ship surrounded by old-fashioned flowers above the inscription *Welcome*.

Length, 3 feet 8 inches; width, 2 feet 6 inches

4 ⁵⁻

156. FLORAL HOOKED RUG

Centre with bouquet, the ends with floral sprays. Worked in soft shades of cream and gray. *Length, 4 feet 10 inches; width, 2 feet 6 inches*

2 0 ⁻

157. FLORAL HOOKED RUG

Sage green ground with regular arrangement of daisies and variegated circular forms enclosing crimson poinsettas.

Length, 6 feet 8 inches; width, 2 feet 5 inches

12 ⁵⁶

158. FLORAL HOOKED RUG

Oval with tan and brown scalloped border enclosing a large bouquet of roses. *Length, 3 feet 5 inches; width, 2 feet 6 inches*

2 ⁵⁻

159. FLORAL HOOKED RUG

Scroll-bordered cartouche enclosing floral forms worked in vermilion and purple. *Length, 4 feet 4 inches; width, 2 feet 2 inches*

12 ⁵⁶

160. MARINE HOOKED RUG

Good Breeze inscribed beneath a rollicking ship riding a choppy sea, the upper corners worked with heads portraying the winds filling the sails of the ship. *Length, 3 feet 9 inches; width, 2 feet 7 inches*

17 ⁵⁶

161. GEOMETRIC HOOKED RUG

Multicolored fish-scale field centring a cartouche containing a large rose.

Length, 5 feet 9 inches; width, 4 feet 4 inches

12 ⁵⁶

162. GEOMETRIC HOOKED RUG

The centre composed of variously colored interlaced bands within a border of circles. *Length, 5 feet 8 inches; width, 5 feet 7 inches*

17 ⁵⁶

163. HOOKED RUNNER

Border of multicolored autumn leaves enclosing a striped centre panel.

Length, 8 feet 1 inch; width, 2 feet 3 inches

2 0 ⁻

[NUMBER 164]

164. MARINE HOOKED RUG

100-

Susan Drew of Salem, fully rigged clipper ship, with sails whipping in the wind, riding a green sea.

Length, 4 feet 10 inches; width, 2 feet 7 inches

[See illustration]

165. STAR AND FLORAL HOOKED RUG

22 56

Soft cream field centred by an eight-pointed star, flanked by floral sprays and smaller stars, scalloped leaf border; worked in shades of red, blue, tan, and green. *Length, 6 feet 2 inches; width, 3 feet 2 inches*

166. GEOMETRIC HOOKED RUG

11 56

Old fashioned stepped pattern worked in grays, tans, mauve, and blue on fawn ground; green-black border. *Length, 6 feet; width, 4 feet 8 inches*

167. GEOMETRIC HOOKED RUG

7 56

Eight large snowflake forms in orange, lavender, black, and buff tipped with yellow on a soft sage ground.

Length, 6 feet 8 inches; width, 2 feet 9 inches

168. TWO PATCHWORK QUILTS

12 56

One worked in squares and triangles of old rose and apple green; the other light blue, worked in squares with eight-pointed stars. Foot corners cut. Worn. *Length, 6 feet 10 inches*

20

169. CURLY MAPLE SLANT-FRONT DESK
Interior fitted with blocked drawers and valanced pigeonholes; case with
four long graduated drawers, bracket feet.
Height, 40½ inches; width, 36 inches

170. SET OF FOUR CARVED WALNUT SIDE CHAIRS
American (?), XVIII Century
Serpentine crest rail, pierced splat, shaped serpentine seat on cabriole legs
connected by H-stretcher. Slip seats covered in gold velvet.

171. CURLY MAPLE TRESTLE TABLE
Rectangular top with cleated ends on vase-shaped trestle supports pierced
by grooved stretcher. *Height, 29 inches; length. 59½ inches*

172. PINE DRESSER *New England, XVIII Century*
Rectangular cabinet, the upper part fitted with two paneled doors over a
lower section containing two similarly paneled large doors; wood knobs.
Height, 6 feet 1 inch; width, 52 inches

173. PINE CHEST OF DRAWERS ON FRAME *New England, XVIII Century*
Case of six graduated drawers on rectangular stand with scalloped apron
carved with three 'scrimshaw' circle motives; duck feet. Stand of later
date. *Height, 55 inches; width, 40 inches*

174. EAGLE CONVEX GILDED WALL MIRROR
Circular molded ball frame surmounted by spread-winged eagle; carved
with scrolls and leafage. *Height, 40 inches; width, 20 inches*

175. PINE SETTLE *New England, XVIII Century*
Small settee with scalloped back and S-scrolled arms; fitted with long
deep drawer and bracket feet. *Length, 44 inches*

176. OAK SIDE TABLE *English, XVII Century*
Rectangular top on frieze containing one small drawer; slender turned
tapering legs joined by H-stretcher.
Height, 27½ inches; length, 42 inches

177. HICKORY, PINE, AND MAPLE COMB-BACK WINDSOR ARMCHAIR
New England, XVIII Century
Well arched back surmounted by serpentine-crested comb; shaped seat,
turned and splayed legs with bulbous H-stretcher. Restored.

178. NEW ENGLAND PINE SAWBUCK DINING TABLE
Rectangular top, trough stretcher, X-supports.
Height, 31 inches; length, 54 inches

179. CARVED MAPLE LOW-POST BEDSTEAD   *New England, XIX Century*
Posts with twisted-rope turning, acorn finials; turned bulbous legs.
2-0- Restored.   *Length, 6 feet 6 inches; width, 45 inches*

180. PINE DOUGH-TRAY TABLE   *Pennsylvania, Late XVIII Century*
Oblong top sliding over a tapered rectangular bin with scalloped apron
/7 ⁵⁶ and turned splayed supports.   *Height, 28 inches; length, 38 inches*

181. CHERRY AND MAPLE CORNER WASHSTAND   *American, XIX Century*
Triangular piece with bowed front, the top pierced for basin, undershelf
/5 - fitted with small drawer.   *Height, 40 inches; width, 23 inches*

182. SHERATON MAHOGANY TWO-PEDESTAL DINING TABLE
One-piece top on vase- and ring-turned pedestals with three outcurved
2 5- grooved legs.   *Height, 29 inches; length, 6 feet*

183. MAHOGANY OCTAGONAL TILTING-TOP TRIPOD STAND   *Sheraton Style*
Vase-turned shaft on cyma-curved tapering legs.
/0-   *Height, 28½ inches; width, 21½ inches*

184. CARVED AND PAINTED CANAPÉ   *Louis XVI Style*
Painted in 'antique' ivory, the rectangular molded frame with closed ends
terminating in fluted quadrangular columns; slightly bowed frontal rail,
4/5 - flaring tapering legs. Loose cushion and two bolsters. Upholstered in
yellow fabric.   *Length, 5 feet 7 inches*

185. CARVED WALNUT OVAL-TOP TABLE   *Italian, XVII Century*
Thumb-molded top overhanging a box-molded frame containing one
/0- drawer; vasiform and collar-turned legs, turned H-stretcher. With
restorations.   *Height, 29 inches; length, 58 inches*

186. SQUARE DECORATED SATINWOOD BREAKFAST TABLE   *Sheraton Style*
Paneled frieze, square tapering legs joined by paneled X-shaped stretchers;
Pan with carved and polychromed floral ornament.
    Height, 30½ inches; length, 42 inches

187. SET OF EIGHT SATINWOOD DECORATED DINING CHAIRS
WITH RUSH SEAT   *Sheraton Style*
50

188. CARVED BEECHWOOD SMALL SETTEE
In the Italian eighteenth century taste; double shield back with lyre splats,
2/5 incurvate arms, fluted square tapering legs. Slip seat in green moire.
    Length, 36 inches

189. CURLY MAPLE CRADLE   *New England, Early XIX Century*
Tapered bin-shaped cradle with unusual scalloped headboard, wings, and
/2 ¹⁵ footboard. Turned egg-shaped finials; shaped rockers. Suitable for log
box.   *Length, 41 inches*

22

[NUMBER 190]

190. THREE-TIER WROUGHT IRON AND WIRE PLANT STAND
                                        American, XIX Century
Rectangular frame supporting three stepped shelves surmounted by a
shaped bower; fitted with casters.
                        Height, 5 feet 9 inches; width, 36 inches

[See illustration]

191. PINE HANGING SHELF   *New England, Early XIX Century*
Three graduated shelves supported by scalloped ends.
                        Height, 36 inches; width, 20½ inches

23

192. PAIR MAHOGANY FOOTSTOOLS   *Empire Style*

Curved rails and legs; tops upholstered in blue and claret-colored flowered fabric.

193. TWO SQUARE MAHOGANY WASHSTANDS

Each fitted with drawer; quadrangular supports.
Heights, 32½ and 30½ inches; widths, 14 and 12½ inches

194. TWO PINE STOOLS   *New England, XIX Century*

One with tripod support, the other with four splayed legs and embroidered seat.   *Height, 18 inches*

195. TWO CANDLESTANDS

One with cross-armed support, on tripod; the other with weighted circular base.   *Heights, 29 and 58 inches*   ·

196. THREE CHAIRS   *New England, XIX Century*

Comprising Windsor armchair, stenciled arrow-back rocker, and painted roundabout chair with upholstered seat. Spindle on armchair broken.

197. PINE HANGING SHELF   *New England, XIX Century*

Three graduated shelves, with scalloped and pierced ends.
Height, 36½ inches; width, 25 inches

198. SET OF FOUR PROVINCIAL OAK SIDE CHAIRS
French, Late XVIII Century

Shaped incurvate back, pierced slat, serpentine seat; fluted quadrangular front legs on spade feet. Seat upholstered in dark green velvet.

199. THREE-TIER WROUGHT IRON AND WIRE PLANT STAND
American, XIX Century

Three oblong stepped shelves with interlaced wire galleries; fitted with casters.   *Height, 37 inches; length, 43 inches*

200. OVAL WROUGHT IRON AND WIRE PLANT STAND
American, XIX Century

Interlaced gallery on oval platform surmounted by stand for òne flowerpot and supported on a diamond-shaped frame with scrolled legs.
Height, 41 inches; width, 30 inches

201. PAIR CAST IRON UPHOLSTERED FOOTSTOOLS   *New York, XIX Century*

Pierced cyma-shaped frames with scroll-foot cabriole legs; retain traces of old gilding. Fitted with denim-upholstered slip seats.
Length, 13 inches

202. WROUGHT IRON FLOWER STAND

Rectangular frame with two circular apertures over a griddle-patterned base.   *Height, 10 inches; length, 18½ inches*

24

[203]   [204]   [203]

203. Pair Connecticut Tin-Mounted Clear Glass Lanterns
Of flattened bulbous form with pierced conical cap. *Height, 16 inches*

[See illustration]

204. Mammoth Tin Signal Lantern
With rayed mirror reflector and fluted smoke vent.
Height, 35¾ inches; width, 20¼ inches

[See illustration]

205. Tin Lantern with Reflector Back and a Brass Ship's Lantern
Ship's lantern shows red, green, and white lights; red glass missing. Accompanied by an iron lion-mask door knocker. Together 3 pieces.

206. Four-gallon Salt-glazed Stoneware Jug
E. & L. P. Norton, Bennington, Vermont
Decorated with floral spray in dark blue. Accompanied by a similar jar, signed NICHOLS AND BOYNTON, BENNINGTON, VERMONT. Together 2 pieces. *Heights, 17 and 13 inches*

25

207. Two Salt-glazed Stoneware Jugs

One decorated with blue butterfly and marked JULIUS NORTON; the other decorated with flower forms in brown and marked L. NORTON AND SON.

Height, 14 inches

208. Two Salt-glazed Stoneware Jars

F. B. Norton & Sons, Worcester, Mass.

One with bird decoration, the other with flower motive, in blue.

Heights, 7½ and 10½ inches

SECOND SESSION

Saturday, February 4, 1939, at 2 p. m.

NUMBERS 209 TO 399 INCLUSIVE

──────────── ☆ ────────────

WATER COLORS

209. TWO WATER COLORS   *Louis C. Tiffany, N.A., American:* 1848-1932
Sir Donald Glacier, B.C., and, on the reverse, Cannon of the Voho.
Signed with initials L. C. T.   *Height, 11¼ inches; width, 8¼ inches*

210. "IT'S REPEAL WE WANT"
Erskine Nicol, R.S.A., A.R.A., English: 1825-1904
Seated near a window an elderly man of intelligent mien has paused dur-
ing the preparation of a thesis, while a copy of 'The Nation', apprising the
spectator of his liberal political leanings, is seen at his right. Signed and
dated 1863 at lower right.   *Height, 12 inches; width, 10 inches*
From the collection of Alderman John Winter

211. TWO WATER COLORS   *Signed, H. P. Spaulding*
Venetian Palace; Dutch Port Scene.
Heights, 21 and 20 inches; widths, 11 and 14½ inches

212. TWO WATER COLORS   *Signed, C. Giorni*
Sunlit Path, with architectural effects; Ploughing with Oxen.
Heights, 15 and 7 inches; widths, 11½ and 20 inches

213. TWO MEXICAN SCENES   *Samuel Colman, N.A., American:* 1832-1920
The Monastery at Hualpa, oil painting on academy board; On the Vega
Canal, water color. Signed.   *Height, 8¼ inches; length, 9 inches*

214. TWO WATER COLORS   *Signed, C. Giorni*
Countryside near Rome; Italian Landscape with Cypresses.
Heights, 12 and 20¼ inches; widths, 25¼ and 10½ inches

215. RUINS OF A CHAPEL   *Samuel Colman, N.A., American:* 1832-1920
In the Indian village of Tlalpam, Mexico; signed at lower right.
Water color: Height, 10½ inches; length, 13½ inches

216. TWO WATER COLORS
Town Beside a Lake, signed H. F. SPAULDING [18]95; Swiss Water
Mill and Cottages.
Heights, 10 and 8¼ inches; widths, 6¾ and 11¼ inches

27

217. THREE LANDSCAPE STUDIES IN PASTELS
/ ᒚ   *Samuel Colman, N.A., American: 1832-1920*
          Ausable Lake, New York; and two moonlight scenes. Signed.
Heights, 11 to 14 inches; lengths, 17½ to 24 inches

218. TWO WATER COLORS
7 ᒚ   The Appian Way, signed LUCIO MARCUACI, Roma 1898; St. Peter's
        from Villa Pamphila Doria, Rome, signed SAB. CAULLI.
Heights, 4½ and 13¾ inches; widths, 11½ and 7½ inches

219. WOODS NEAR ROME   ·   *Signed, C. Giorni*
/ ᒚ   Gnarled trees with scant foliage rising from field of grasses and rocks with
        distant view of blue mountains.
Water color: Height, 24¼ inches; length, 38 inches

220. TWO WATER COLORS   *Signed, C. Giorni* ·
        Villa Gateway; Ruins of an Aqueduct.
7 ᒚ   *Heights, 20 and 9¼ inches; widths, 10¾ and 19¾ inches*

221. ENTRANCE TO AN ITALIAN MUSEUM   *Signed, E. Bensa*
        A wall at right covered with carved coats of arms and a balcony featuring
oal   the façade straight ahead.   *Height, 23½ inches; width, 15½ inches*

222. TWO PASTELS   *Samuel Colman, N.A., American: 1832-1920*
        California Landscape at Sunset; Point Lobos, Monterey. Signed.
                           Height, 8 inches; length, 9 inches
/2 ᒚ   *Height, 13 inches; length, 18¼ inches*

223. THREE WATER COLORS   *Samuel Colman, N.A., American: 1832-1920*
        Twilight at Lake George; Gill Brook in the Adirondacks; Point Lobos,
/ ᒚ   Monterey. Signed.   *Heights, 8 to 17 inches; widths, 10 to 11 inches*

224. AN ARAB ENCAMPMENT   *Signed, E. Kilbourne Foote, 1903*
        Against a background of palms and sunset sky are seen a number of figures
        among tents, with goats and fowl about.
22 ᒚ   *Height, 17 inches; length, 26½ inches*

225. THREE PASTELS   *Samuel Colman, N.A., American: 1832-1920*
        Twilight with Evening Star; Mountain Lake Scene with Cattle; and
/ ᒚ   Late Afternoon, Point Lobos, Monterey, California.
Heights, 12½ to 17¼ inches; lengths, 14¼ to 19 inches

226. SPRING IN VENICE   *Henry Pember Smith, American: 1854-1907*
        A boatman is maneuvering his rowboat in a limpid blue canal which is
/2 ᒚ   bordered by delightful Gothic Palaces and foliage in pink and white blos-
        soms; signed at lower left.
Water color: Height, 21¼ inches; width, 14¾ inches

227. TWO PASTELS   *Samuel Colman, N.A., American:* 1832-1920
   A Bit of California's Coast, with Indians in a canoe in the foreground;
   Colorado Canyon. Both signed.
                                 Height, 14¾ inches; length, 17½ inches
                                 Height, 13¾ inches; length, 13½ inches

228. TWO WATER COLORS   *Signed, H. P. Spaulding*
   Landscape: A Gray Day; Dutch Mill.
                      Heights, 13¾ and 21¼ inches; lengths, 21 and 15 inches

OIL PAINTINGS

229. BROWN RACEHORSE IN PASTURE   *R. Goubie, French: XIX Century*
   Signed at lower right and dated 1883.
                                 Height, 19 inches; length, 23 inches

230. THE RACEHORSE PRINCESS MORELL
                        J. W. Johnson, Contemporary American
   Carefully delineated portrait of a chestnut horse; landscape background.
                                 Height, 20 inches; length, 24 inches

231. TWO LANDSCAPES
   French scene, signed ADRIEN DUMONT; sunset landscape, signed EDWARD
   GAY, N.A.   *Panels: Height, 7 inches; length, 9½ inches*
                                 Height, 8 inches; length, 10½ inches

232. PORTRAIT OF A LADY OF THE MAUVE DECADE;
   WINTER SCENE WITH DUCKS
   Signed J. HAGAMAN, Paris 1895, and FRITZ LANGE '71' respectively.
                            Panels: Height, 11 inches; width, 8 inches
                                 Height, 6 inches; length, 8 inches

233. THE CARES OF MOTHERHOOD   *Leon Caille, French: XIX Century*
   A young mother in peasant costume has a sleeping baby on her knee while
   she helps her daughter with her lessons.
                                 Height, 36 inches; width, 25 inches

234. INTERIOR OF A CHURCH
                     Pieter Neeffs the Younger, Flemish: 1620-1675
   View looking down the nave supported by round columns and Gothic
   arches; the sun shines through the clerestory onto a tessellated floor.
                            Panel: Height, 13½ inches; length, 17 inches
   Collection of Prince Alexander of Georgia, St. Petersburg

235. MADONNA AND CHILD; HEAD OF AN ORIENTAL WOMAN
   Signed F. DE ZURBARAN at upper right; signed W. BLACKMAN.
                            Panels: Height, 13¼ inches; width, 9 inches
                                 Height, 10 inches; width, 8 inches

29

236. TWO OIL PAINTINGS   *Samuel Colman, N.A., American: 1832-1920*
Edge of the Wood at Irvington-on-Hudson; Marine. Signed.

10
                            Height, 6¾ inches; length, 12¾ inches
                            Height, 14¼ inches; length, 16½ inches

237. LAKE LANDSCAPE   *J. F. Kensett, N.A., American: 1818-1872*
Signed at lower left, JFK.   *Height, 14 inches; length, 24 inches*

238. LANDSCAPE WITH CATTLE
Undulating expanse with a brook and cows. Signed, GEORGE INNESS
1864.   · *Height, 14 inches; length, 24 inches*

239. TWO OIL PAINTINGS
Temple of Philae on the Nile by Louis C. Tiffany; On the Guadalquivir,
Spain, by Samuel Colman, N.A., signed.
                      Height, 8 inches; length, 12 inches
                      Height, 5½ inches; length, 9¼ inches

240. MEXICAN LANDSCAPE   *Samuel Colman, N.A., American: 1832-1920*
A stream winds its way toward an arched bridge, by a group of buildings
at the left. Signed at lower right. *Height, 9¾ inches; length, 13½ inches*

241. TWO OIL PAINTINGS   *Samuel Colman, N.A., American: 1832-1920*
Zacatecas and Marfil, Mexico.   *Height, 7¾ inches; length, 8 inches*
                      Height, 8¼ inches; length, 9¼ inches

242. MARKET PLACE IN A BELGIAN TOWN, AND BATTLE SCENE
Painted circle, signed P. JOHNSON, 1817; the other signed PH. WOU-
WERMAN.   *Panels: 8½ inches square*
                      Height, 6 inches; length, 7¾ inches

243. TWO OIL PAINTINGS   *Samuel Colman, N.A., American: 1832-1920*
Dutch Coast Scene, with cottages and windmills; Afternoon on the
Rhine. Signed at lower right.   *Height, 15 inches; length, 19¼ inches*
                      Height, 12 inches; length, 19¼ inches

244. RUGGED COAST IN SCOTLAND
A lone fisherman is halting on a path in the foreground as he looks at a
yawl in the bay at the right. Signed at lower left, MACMASTER.
                      Height, 12 inches; length, 18 inches

245. PAIR FLOWER PAINTINGS   *French School: XVIII Century*
Colorful flowers in basket on a marble pedestal.
          Academy board: Height, 16¾ inches; width, 13¾ inches

246. PAIR FLOWER PAINTINGS   *French: Early XVIII Century*
Autumn flowers in vase on a table; dark background.
                      Height, 16½ inches; width, 13 inches

247. STILL LIFE   *Signed, Fred Grant Young*
Dish, flask of wine, oranges, and books in nice arrangement.
                 Height, 16 inches; length, 24 inches

248. THE APERITIF   *Charles Chaplin, French: 1825-1891*
A comely maid gazes at the spectator as she passes with a platter with a carafe of sherry and glasses. Signed at *lower* right.
              Height, 31½ inches; width, 19 inches

249. PAIR STILL-LIFE PAINTINGS   *French: XVIII Century*
Representing pomegranates, figs, grapes, melons, mushrooms, and flower sprays.   *Height, 19¼ inches; length, 25 inches*

250. BELGIAN TOWN SCENE
Signed, P. G. VATINS, 1866.
          Panel: Height, 13½ inches; width, 11 inches

251. BARNYARD FOWL   *L. Julliard, French: XIX Century*
Signed at *lower* left and dated 1865.
             Height, 10 inches; length, 14 inches

252. THE TWO CRONIES   *Carl Hirschberg, American: 1854-1923*
Two bright youngsters are keeping each other company in a garden. Signed at lower left.   *Height, 22 inches; length, 28 inches*

253. SADDLEHORSE IN STABLE
A fine dark-brown horse, his bridle fastened to a ring on the wall. Signed LYNWOOD PALMEN, 1891.   *Height, 18 inches; length, 24 inches*

254. LIFE ON THE FARM   *Charles Emile Jacque, French: 1813-1894*
An old sow and other porkers, with fowl sharing the pen; an elderly peasant woman comes forward with the rations. Fine light effect from top window. Signed at lower left.   *Height, 18 inches; width, 15 inches*

255. BARNYARD FOWL; DUTCH INTERIOR
The first signed E. J. VERBOECKHOVEN; the second depicts peasants at their frugal meal and is signed K. F. VENNEMAN 1840.
       Panels: Height, 10½ inches; length, 11¾ inches
            Height, 12 inches; length, 16 inches

256. TWO OIL PAINTINGS   *Samuel Colman, N.A., American: 1832-1920*
Rocky Coast; Sunset Glow, signed at lower right.
       Height, 16 inches; length, 19½ inches
       Height, 10 inches; length, 21 inches

257. NEW ENGLAND COUNTRYSIDE
A lake at the right and a lumberman with logging team at the left. Signed, E. L. HENRY.   *Height, 16 inches; length, 20 inches*

258. AUTUMN SCENE   *Samuel Colman, N.A., American: 1832-1920*

Cattle are wading in a shallow stream which traverses a yellow field; fine trees in autumn foliage under a blue and gray sky. Signed at lower right.

Panel: Height, 9 inches; length, 11 inches

259. LANDSCAPE

Late afternoon effect. Signed, GEORGE INNESS.

Height, 12 inches; length, 16¼ inches

260. PASTORALE   *Nicolas Berchem, Dutch: 1620-1683*

Cows, a goat, and a sheep, with their shepherd, a dog, and two peasants are grouped about the foreground. Hilly country with a stream winding at the right; gray and cloudy sky.

Panel: Height, 15½ inches; width, 20½ inches

261. ITALIAN SCENE   *Signed, E. Kilbourne Foote, 1904*

A couple of long-horned white oxen are drawing a cart along a narrow road with a palace with artistic tower in the distance.

Height, 19¾ inches; width, 13 inches

262. ROMAN RUINS   *School of Pagnini, Italian: XVIII Century*

Height, 24 inches; length, 29 inches

263. PETRARCH AND LAURA   *Joseph Cosenza, Italian: XIX Century*

Depicted after their meeting in the Church of S. Claire. Signed and dated 1861.

Height, 18¼ inches; width, 14¼ inches

264. PORTRAIT DRAWING   *French School, XIX Century*

Full-length figure, seated, in the academic robes of an artist, holding a tablet and pencil. Signed at lower right, JEAN AUGUSTE DOMINIQUE INGRES.

Height, 8¼ inches; width, 6¼ inches

265. TWO OIL PAINTINGS   *Samuel Colman, N.A., American: 1832-1920*

Italian Scene with Pilgrims at Shrine; Fishing Boats Beached at Etretat. Signed.

Height, 11¾ inches; length, 17¾ inches
Height, 7¼ inches; length, 10¾ inches

266. INTERIOR OF A WOOD
Narcisse Virgile Diaz de la Peña, French: 1812-1876
Tree trunks rising from lush foreground with several silvery touches of light filtering through the foliage. Signed at lower right.
Cradled panel: Height, 9¼ inches; width, 14½ inches

267. MODERN GILT ALTARPIECE: MADONNA AND CHILD
With water-color and gouache miniature after Gerard David. On dark velvet base.
Size over all: Height, 9 inches; width, 10 inches

268. ANNUNCIATION TO THE SHEPHERDS
Nicolas Berchem, Dutch: 1620-1683
Under a cloudy blue sky with the full moon at left, a burst of heavenly light at right illumines the figure of an angel appearing to the shepherds kneeling in awe by a cottage. In the rocky foreground is a group of goats and cattle.
Panel: Height, 17¼ inches; width, 14¼ inches
Collection of Alexander Arensberg, Esq., London

269. THE MERCENARY MARRIAGE
German School, XVI Century
Seated at a table before a dark background is a group of seven figures, the young bride in crimson cap and robe embracing the bridegroom, who is about to place a ring upon the finger of her left hand, which rests upon a bag of gold. At right, a man holds an open jewel casket, from which he has taken a crucifix.
Panel: Height, 22 inches; length, 33¼ inches
Collection of Alexander Arensberg, Esq., London

270. VENUS AND CUPID
Venetian School, XVI Century
Three-quarter-length standing figure of Venus with long golden hair, wearing a richly brocaded robe. Her right hand rests upon the back of curly-haired Cupid, who nestles at her side.
Height, 41 inches; width, 31 inches
From the Bevilacqua family of Verona
Second National Loan Exhibition, Grosvenor Gallery, London, 1913-4

271. COPY AFTER REMBRANDT'S SELF-PORTRAIT
A. Guerrieri, Florence
Height, 28½ inches; width, 22½ inches

AMERICAN AND ENGLISH FURNITURE
AND DECORATIONS

272. BRISTOL PINK GLASS LAMP
Ormolu-mounted, and fitted for electricity.   *Height, 29 inches*

273. VICTORIAN POTTERY BEDROOM SET
Comprising large bowl and pitcher, soap dish with cover, small pitcher, and mug. Decorated with floral forms on a rose ground.

274. FRENCH PORCELAIN CLOCK
Decorated with lady and courtier in colored enamels, having ormolu side brackets and chain. Accompanied by a Minton china tile with bird decoration, mounted with ormolu as a tray. Together 2 pieces.
Diameter of clock, 8 inches; length of tray, 13 inches

275. BENNINGTON PARIAN WARE BUST OF SHAKESPEARE
Mid-XIX Century
Height, 16 inches

276. TWENTY MAUVE-DECORATED DUTCH TILES
With various views of houses and castles.   *5 inches square*

277. BRONZE AMERICAN INDIAN GROUP
Depicting an American Indian warrior seated in a canoe, with dead game at his feet. Signed DUCHOISELLE.   *Height, 25 inches; length, 41 inches*
Collection of Samuel Insull, American Art Association-Anderson Galleries, Inc., 1936

278. CARVED MAHOGANY PIECRUST TRIPOD STAND   *Chippendale Style*
Ribbon-carved edge, turned and spirally carved shaft, leaf-and husk-carved cabriole legs terminating in claw and ball feet.
Height, 24½ inches; diameter, 17¾ inches

279. CHIPPENDALE CARVED MAHOGANY AND GILDED WALL MIRROR
Rectangular frame with carved fruit and leaf pendants surmounted by a pierced crest with carved scrolls and phoenix finial.
Height, 49 inches; width, 23½ inches

280. CHIPPENDALE CARVED MAHOGANY AND GILDED WALL MIRROR
Matching the preceding.   *Height, 50 inches; width, 21 inches*

281. HEPPLEWHITE MAHOGANY AND CHERRY CHEST OF DRAWERS
American, XIX Century
Deep drawer with veneer-paneled front above three shallow drawers; half-round reeded uprights, short turned legs and brass feet, brass knobs. Restored.   *Height, 49 inches; width, 47 inches*

282. LOUIS XVI BLACK AND GOLD LACQUER SEWING STAND
Composed of a coffret with a hinged lid on a stand with flaring legs and undershelf; simulating Chinese lacquer.
Height, 32 inches; width, 17 inches

PINE CHEST OF DRAWERS
Paneled ends, scalloped valance, bracket feet; wood knobs.
Height, 34¾ inches; length, 38¼ inches

VICTORIAN LACQUERED SEWING TABLE   *American, XIX Century*
Hinged paneled top disclosing compartmented frieze over a sliding
drawer; turned legs, trestle support connected by turned and bulbous
stretchers. With scroll, floral, and bird decoration.
Height, 26 inches; width, 16 inches

MAHOGANY CARVED AND GILDED MANTEL MIRROR
With scrolled crest surmounted by spread eagle.
Height, 34 inches; length, 5 feet 1 inch

CARVED MAHOGANY SMALL SOFA   *Duncan Phyfe Style*
Reeded crest rail, rolled arms with curved supports running into reeded
seat rail, carved cornucopia-shaped legs with brass paw tips. Upholstered
in black leatherette.   *Length, 5 feet 2 inches*

FIGURED MAHOGANY TILTING-TOP TRIPOD TABLE
In Duncan Phyfe style, with shaped rectangular top on vase-turned shaft;
outcurved legs resting on ball feet.
Height, 28½ inches; width, 26 inches

NEW ENGLAND CHERRY CHEST OF DRAWERS
Four drawers with beaded edge, fluted quarter-round columns, molded
base and bracket feet.   *Height, 36 inches; length, 40¾ inches*

HEPPLEWHITE CURLY MAPLE SMALL SIDEBOARD
New England, XIX Century
With arched centre section containing one drawer, flanked by two deep
drawers between square tapering legs with spade feet.
Height, 39¼ inches; length, 5 feet 2¼ inches

SHERATON INLAID MAHOGANY AND MAPLE WORK TABLE
Square top crossbanded in contrasting darker wood over a frieze containing two inlaid maple drawers; undershelf with scalloped gallery; turned,
reeded, and tapered legs.   *Height, 28½ inches; width, 15 inches*

SHERATON INLAID MAHOGANY AND MAPLE WORK TABLE
Matching the preceding.   *Height, 28½ inches; width, 15 inches*

[NUMBER 292]

292. HEPPLEWHITE INLAID APPLEWOOD CHEST OF DRAWERS
New England, circa 1785
Oblong top, edge inlaid with checkered light and dark wood; four drawers, valanced skirt and French feet. Old oval brasses.
Height, 34 inches; length, 39 inches

[See illustration]

293. MAHOGANY DISH-TOP TRIPOD STAND   *Sheraton Style*
Circular top with molded edge, vase-turned shaft and cyma-curved legs ending in spade feet.   *Height, 27¼ inches; diameter, 16¼ inches*

294. CARVED AND GILDED MIRROR   *Sheraton Style*
Molded cornice with pendent spherical balls on concave pilasters centring a twisted rope carving enclosing a mirror surmounted by a painted glass panel showing a house in mountainous countryside.
Height, 33¾ inches; width, 21¼ inches

295. MAHOGANY BEDSIDE TABLE   *Sheraton Style*
Square top on ring- and vase-turned legs enclosing shelf containing one drawer fitted with ivory knobs.   *Height, 26 inches; width, 15¾ inches*

36

296. MAHOGANY THREE-TIER TRIPOD DUMB-WAITER   *Chippendale Style*
Three trays with molded edge on vase- and ring-turned shaft and cabriole
legs terminating in snake feet.   *Height, 39 inches; diameter, 23½ inches*

297. PAIR FRET-CARVED MAHOGANY TRIPOD STANDS   *Hepplewhite Style*
Octagonal top with fret-carved gallery on turned shaft and splayed legs.
                              Height, 24¾ inches; diameter, 16 inches

298. PAIR OVAL PEDESTAL MIRRORS   *New York, XIX Century*
Openwork gilded metal oval frame held by ladies in Colonial costume on
pedestal flanked by American flag and shield.
                              Height, 21 inches; width, 14¼ inches

299. INLAID MAHOGANY BOW-FRONT SMALL CHEST OF DRAWERS
Top edged with checkered inlay above four cockbeaded graduated drawers
with satinwood paneled centres; splayed feet.
                              Height, 31½ inches; width, 27½ inches

300. AMERICAN WALNUT CLAW-AND-BALL-FOOT TRIPOD TABLE
With molded circular tilting top on bird cage; turned shaft and cabriole
legs.   *Height, 30 inches; diameter, 34 inches*

301. CARVED MAHOGANY TALL-POST BED   *Sheraton Style*
Full size bed in the McIntire taste, with shaped headboard placed between turned headposts; footposts reeded and carved with acanthus and
tasseled drapery motives. Urn-shaped finials.
        Height, 5 feet 10¾ inches; length, 6 feet 8 inches; width, 5 feet

302. SHERATON INLAID MAHOGANY AND SATINWOOD TAMBOUR
       SECRETARY DESK
The upper section consisting of a bow-front compartment containing two
shallow drawers over a central hinged cupboard flanked by reeded shutter
compartments concealing small drawers and pigeonholes; the lower part
with hinged writing flap over three long graduated drawers; square tapered legs. Drawer fronts, writing flaps, and panels in branch satinwood;
lion brass bail handles.   *Height, 46½ inches; length, 34½ inches*

37

303. CARVED MAHOGANY BLOCK-FRONT BONNET-TOP CHEST ON CHEST
In the Rhode Island taste; the upper part with molded cyma-curved pediment terminating in carved rosace above a case containing three small shell-carved drawers over four long drawers; lower section consisting of four long drawers on molded base with claw and ball feet. Supplied with scrolled Chippendale style brasses, bail handles.

Height, 7 feet; width, 38 inches

[See illustration]

304. GEORGIAN MAHOGANY DRUM TABLE
Circular table with gilt crimson tooled leather inset over a paneled frieze with four drawers; carved shaft with leaf-carved and reeded quadrangular support, shod and castered.   *Height, 29½ inches; diameter, 30 inches*

305. SHERATON MAHOGANY HARPSICHORD
Muzio Clementi and Company, London, Early XIX Century
Long rectangular vase with hinged top; keyboard panel of nicely figured and decorated sycamore. Inscribed *New Patent, Muzio Clementi & Co—Cheapside, London.* Front, top, and ends paneled with ebonized stringing; seven turned tapering legs with *bronze doré* collars and casters.

Height, 31½ inches; length, 5 feet 7 inches

TAPESTRIES

306. TWO FLEMISH VERDURE TAPESTRY FRAGMENTS   *XVIII Century*
One circular, the other rectangular.   *Diameter, 42 inches*

Height, 1 foot 11 inches; length, 3 feet

307. EMPIRE TAPESTRY   *French, circa 1800*
Two classical figures with dog in a park landscape with ruins in the background; floral and fruit border. Woven in brown, red, blue, and yellow.

Height, 7 feet; width, 5 feet

38

[NUMBER 303]

308. IMPORTANT RENAISSANCE TAPESTRY   *Brussels, XVI Century*
THE BUILDING OF THE TEMPLE OF BABYLON. In the foreground, six figures of masons chiseling, laying mortar, and lifting blocks of stone are
shown against a background of rich verdure in green and yellow; in the
upper centre an artisan is seen receiving a scroll from a saintly figure
enveloped in clouds. The whole enclosed in a wide border of birds, fruits,
flowers, and leaves. The tapestry is finely woven with silk in rich tones
of green, yellow, blue, and red. Outer border slightly worn.

Height, 11 feet 3 inches; width, 10 feet

Note: This tapestry, which is in remarkably good condition, is an
important and very rare example of the period, particularly fine in color
and design.

[See illustration]

[NUMBER 308]

309. IMPORTANT AUBUSSON TAPESTRY   *French, Early XVIII Century*
THE ADORATION OF THE MAGI. The *Infant* Christ held by His Mother
is surrounded by a group of figures inside a ruined building. In the foreground are the Three Wise Men of the *East*, Caspar, Melchior, and
Balthasar, with attendants and a Roman soldier carrying shield and staff;
two attendants and two camels in the background. The blue sky can be
seen through a break in the masonry. Border of fruits and flowers.
Woven in rich shades of green, yellow, brown, red, and ivory. Woven in
the lower selvage, M R D AVBVSSON I·C.

Height, 9 feet 3 inches; length, 17 feet

Note: This tapestry is in excellent condition and beautiful in color.

[See illustration]

TRANSCASPIAN RUGS

310. YOMUD RUG
With latchhooked rhombs in dark reds, blue, white, and orange on dark
plum field; four geometrical borders, two symbolical borders at the ends.

Length, 10 feet; width, 6 feet 9 inches

311. YOMUD RUG
Red-brown ground with latchhooked rhombs in tile red, orange, green,
white, and blue; three geometrical borders, two symbolical borders at the
ends.   *Length, 10 feet 5 inches; width, 5 feet 11 inches*

312. SHIRAZ RUG
Herati lattice pattern in green, cream, white, blue, yellow, black, and
brown on a tile red field; nine vine and floral borders.

Length, 13 feet 2 inches; width, 6 feet 2 inches

313. PAIR SEREBEND RUGS
Tile red field with multicolored pears in allover pattern; ten geometrical,
floral, and 'lace' borders, in blue, brown, cream, and red.

Length, 6 feet 2 inches; widths, 4 feet 3 inches and 4 feet 5 inches

314. YOMUD TURKOMAN RUG
Large geometrical diamond forms on wine red ground, in blue, brown,
and white; three ornamental borders, two symbolical borders at the ends.

Length, 9 feet 5 inches; width, 5 feet 5 inches

315. BALUCHISTAN RUG
Ornamented diamond-shaped medallions on a plum field, in blue, white,
and brown; three geometrical borders, ornamented ends.

Length, 7 feet 8 inches; width, 5 feet 5 inches

316. YOMUD RUG
Geometrical diamonds on a deep plum field, in red, dark blue, green, and
cream; three geometrical borders, two at the ends.

Length, 9 feet 11 inches; width, 6 feet 5 inches

317. TEKKE TURKOMAN RUG

Rows of shaped ovals and geometrical forms in brown, white, and blue on a tile red field; many geometrical, floral, and ornamental borders; two geometrical borders at the ends.

Length, 9 feet 6 inches; width, 7 feet 1 inch

[See illustration]

318. AFGHAN RUG

Cerise field with shaped oval medallions interspersed with geometrical signs; three geometrical borders, in blue, orange, and brown.

Length, 9 feet 11 inches; width, 8 feet 10 inches

319. YOMUD BOKHARA RUG

Violet plum field with latchhooked diamond forms in blue, orange, red, brown, and white; five complementary borders, two ornamental borders at the ends. *Length, 9 feet 6 inches; width, 5 feet 11 inches*

320. SEREBEND RUG

Deep rose field with allover design of multicolored flame motives; eleven floral and 'lace' borders in green, blue, brown, and cream.

Length, 10 feet 6 inches; width, 7 feet 3 inches

321. YOMUD RUG

Plum field with latchhooked diamond forms in white, red, blue, and brown; three geometrical borders, and two 'tree' ends.

Length, 10 feet 2 inchs; width, 5 feet 9 inches

322. TEKKE TURKOMAN RUG

Rows of shaped medallions in blue, white, and tile red on a mulberry field; seven geometrical borders, two at the ends.

Length, 10 feet; width, 7 feet 9 inches

323. YOMUD BOKHARA RUG

Rows of shaped ovals interspersed with geometrical diamond forms; fourteen geometrical borders, two geometrical borders at the ends; all in blue, white, and tile red on a red-brown ground.

Length, 10 feet 3 inches; width, 7 feet 4 inches

324. YOMUD-HATSCHLU RUG

Allover floral design in white, blue, and red in four parts on violet ground; different ornamental, geometrical, and floral borders, one end with ornamental design. *Length, 5 feet 6 inches; width, 4 feet 4 inches*

325. YOMUD TURKOMAN RUG

Similar to the preceding on a red-brown ground, in blue, brown, and cream; three geometrical borders.

Length, 10 feet 1 inch; width, 6 feet 6 inches

[NUMBER 317]

326. YOMUD RUG

10 5- Violet ground with latchhooked rhombs in tile red, blue, yellow, and white; five geometrical and ornamental borders, two geometrical borders at the ends. *Length, 11 feet 6 inches; width, 7 feet 2 inches*

327. TEKKE TURKOMAN RUG

150 Rows of shaped medallions in orange, blue, and red on a wine crimson field; seven geometrical borders, two at the ends. *Length, 11 feet 4 inches; width, 7 feet 9 inches*

328. KASHAN RUG

2 15 Shaped floral medallion on a field of similar shape, spandrels with trees and rosettes, and allover vine and flower design on tile red ground with design in yellow, cream, blue, brown, and green; ten vine and flower borders. *Length, 11 feet; width, 7 feet 6 inches*

[See illustration]

329. YOMUD TURKOMAN RUG

80 Red-brown ground with rows of medallions in blue, red, white, and brown; seven geometrical borders, two at the ends. *Length, 9 feet 7 inches; width, 6 feet 10 inches*

330. YOMUD BOKHARA RUG

200 Rows of octagons with animal decoration and geometrical figures, in orange, blue, cream, green, and yellow on wine red field; seven geometrical borders. *Length, 14 feet 10 inches; width, 8 feet 5 inches*

331. YOMUD TURKOMAN RUG

90- Octagonal medallions with geometrical edge, in dark and light blue, brown, black, and white on a wine red ground; eleven geometrical and floral borders, two symbolical borders at the ends. *Length, 11 feet 10 inches; width, 6 feet 10 inches*

AMERICAN AND ENGLISH FURNITURE
AND DECORATIONS [CONCLUDED]

332. GEORGIAN SILK-EMBROIDERED NEEDLEWORK PICTURE

English, Early XIX Century

35- Depicting a scene from the New Testament; worked in soft shades of red, blue, brown, and gray. Ebonized frame.

Height, 22 inches; length, 26 inches

333. PAIR CARVED MAHOGANY EAGLE WALL BRACKETS

22 16 Trefoil tops supported by carved spread eagle.

Height, 18 inches; width, 16 inches

334. PINE LAP WRITING DESK   *New England, Early XIX Century*

10- Containing drawer with divisions for paper, quills, and ink. Accompanied by a curly maple stationery rack with removable partition.

Length of writing desk, 18 inches; height of rack, 8¾ inches

[NUMBER 328]

335. SHELL-INLAID AMBOYNA WOOD TEA CADDY

English, Early XIX Century

Accompanied by a maple pipe box. Together 2 pieces.

Height of tea caddy, 5 inches; length, 9½ inches
Height of pipe box, 17½ inches

336. MOTHER-OF-PEARL INLAID MAHOGANY TRAVELING CASE

English, Early XIX Century

Plush-lined compartmented interior fitted with glass jars and bottles, and having secret jewel drawer in base released by pin in side.

Height, 7 inches; length, 11 inches

337. PINE AND OAK CHILD'S HIGHBOY   *New England, XVIII Century*

The upper section consisting of a rectangular case with two small and two long drawers; lower part with molded edge and deep frieze containing two small deep drawers, arched and scalloped apron, turned tapering legs with ball feet. Restored.   *Height, 36 inches; width, 23 inches*

338. CHIPPENDALE CARVED MAHOGANY TILTING-TOP TABLE

Octagonal top with acanthus-carved scalloped edge tilting on bird cage; turned and carved baluster shaft and acanthus-carved tripod support with claw and ball feet.   *Height, 29 inches; diameter, 22½ inches*

339. CARVED MAHOGANY COFFEE TABLE   *Chinese Chippendale Style*

Rectangular scalloped tray top on fret-carved square legs with pierced brackets and H-stretcher.   *Height, 20 inches; length, 28 inches*

340. GEORGIAN DECORATED LACQUER LADY'S DRESSING CABINET ON STAND

English, XIX Century

Rectangular boxed dressing case with hinged flaps, enclosing numerous compartments in front of an upright cabinet with double-paneled doors; the latter, in turn, enclose drawers and compartments and are surmounted by a broken-arch pediment. On stand with cabriole legs and paw feet. The whole piece lacquered in the Chinese taste, painted with flowers and domestic scenes.   *Height, 5 feet 5 inches; width, 25 inches*

341. CARVED MAHOGANY TRIPOD DRUM TABLE   *Sheraton Style*

Revolving tooled and gilded red leather-covered circular top with four drawers in apron; vase-turned shaft and reeded splayed legs having brass paw tips.   *Height, 28 inches; diameter, 29¾ inches*

342. ASH FRIEZÉ-UPHOLSTERED WING CHAIR

New England, XVIII Century

Slightly arched back, serpentine and splayed wings, rolled arms, quadrangular legs with box stretchers; loose seat cushion. Upholstered in floral-patterned friezé with green ground.

48

[NUMBER 343]

343. INLAID MAHOGANY TAMBOUR DESK   *Hepplewhite Style*
Upper section with tambour shutters enclosing pigeonholes and small
drawers flanking a central cupboard; lower section with folding baize-
lined writing flap above two long drawers. Quadrangular tapering legs
inlaid with ebony and satinwood striped panels and husk motives.

Height, 45½ inches; width, 36½ inches

[See illustration]

344. INLAID MAHOGANY CHEST OF DRAWERS   *Hepplewhite Style*
Rectangular top with inlaid edge, on a case of four drawers of graduated
depth having cockbeaded molding and crossbanded border; shaped valance,
centring an inlaid satinwood oval, running into French feet. Furnished
with a set of eagle brasses.   *Height, 36¼ inches; width, 35¼ inches*

49

345. GEORGIAN INLAID MAHOGANY KNEEHOLE DESK
Small writing desk with oblong molded top, decorated with satinwood
paterae and crossbanding; frieze containing one long drawer. Pedestals,
each with three small drawers, flanking a central section containing a recessed urn-inlaid cupboard. All inlaid with scrolls and husks in satinwood; molded base, bracket feet. *Height, 31 inches; length, 35 inches*

346. EMPIRE MAHOGANY TALL-CASE CLOCK
Glazed front and side panels, three-quarter-round pilasters supporting
arched molded pediment; bracket feet. *Height, 7 feet 10 inches*

347. GEORGIAN INLAID MAHOGANY SLANT-FRONT DESK
Hinged writing flap with oval crotch mahogany medallion enclosing a
fitted interior; the case with four long drawers faced with stringing.
Molded base, bracket feet. *Height, 40½ inches; width, 37 inches*

348. CARVED AND INLAID MAHOGANY GRANDMOTHER'S CLOCK
Small case with carved swanneck pediment supported by slender colonettes
enclosing a glazed door with painted dial and rocking ship; case containing one long door with reeded quarter-round pilasters. Box-paneled base
with ogee bracket feet. *Height, 59 inches*

349. CHIPPENDALE CARVED MAHOGANY WALL MIRROR
Upright molded frame with pierced and scrolled pediment centring a
carved and gilded phoenix. *Height, 40 inches; width, 24 inches*

[See illustration]

350. MAHOGANY BLOCK-FRONT SLANT-TOP DESK
Rectangular case with hinged slant writing flap enclosing a fitted interior
of drawers and pigeonholes over a blocked front with four graduated
drawers; claw and ball feet. Chippendale style brass bail handles.
Height, 41 inches; width, 39 inches

[See illustration]

351. HEPPLEWHITE INLAID MAHOGANY SERPENTINE CHEST OF DRAWERS
Molded cyma-curved top on case of four drawers, each centred with
branch satinwood panel and crossbanded in satinwood; valanced skirt,
splayed feet. Lion brass bail handles.
Height, 35 inches; length, 38½ inches

352. CARVED MAHOGANY LOWBOY
In the Philadelphia taste; molded oblong top with indented corners, over
one long drawer and three smaller drawers, the central one shell-carved,
flanked by quarter-round pilasters; valanced skirt, leaf-carved cabriole legs
with claw and ball feet. *Height, 31 inches; length, 34 inches*

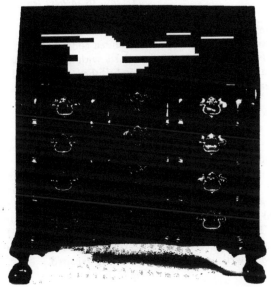

[NUMBERS 349 AND 350]

353. SHERATON MAHOGANY AND SATINWOOD UPHOLSTERED SOFA
In the Salem taste; slightly arched back and cyma-shaped closed ends extending into paneled arms with reeded and bulbous supports; satinwood paneled dies, turned tapered and reeded front legs. Upholstered in crimson velvet.

Length, 5 feet 6 inches

354. SET OF EIGHT CHIPPENDALE CARVED MAHOGANY DINING CHAIRS
Comprising two armchairs and six side chairs; serpentine crest rail carved with acanthus, pierced vasiform splat with carved ribbon and leafage. Molded tapering seat; cabriole legs, carved at the knee, ending in claw and ball feet. Slip seats upholstered in mauve and tan damask.

355. AMERICAN MAHOGANY AND SATINWOOD INLAID SERPENTINE SIDEBOARD
In the Hepplewhite taste; overhanging cyma-fronted top, on frieze containing one long drawer and two short drawers below which are hinged cupboards. The recessed central section contains paneled double doors; square tapering legs. With brass pulls.

Height, 38 inches; length, 5 feet 6 inches

356. GEORGIAN CARVED MAHOGANY THREE-PART DINING TABLE
Comprising a central section with voluted and carved baluster shaft, scroll- and leaf-carved quadrangular supports with claw and ball feet, and two semi-oval end sections similarly embellished with tripod supports. Two extra leaves.

Height, 30 inches; length extended, 12 feet; width, 47 inches

357. QUEEN ANNE CHERRY BONNET-TOP HIGHBOY

New England, circa 1750

The upper section is a case of four long drawers above which are three small ones. The full bonnet top in broken-arch pattern is completely outlined in voluted moldings surrounding the looped aperture filled by a slender plinth. The lower section contains five drawers, one enriched with a carved shell, a similar motive being repeated on the small centre drawer above. The triple-arched skirt is recessed at the centre. The piece stands on Dutch-footed cabriole legs, bears its original set of willow brass handles, and is well patinated. One rear leg repaired.

Height, 6 feet 11 inches; width, 39 inches

358. GEORGIAN CARVED MAHOGANY PEDESTAL DESK
Oblong top paneled with gilded crimson tooled leather, twisted-rope carved edge; supported by two pedestals, each face of which contains four drawers, flanking a frieze containing one drawer. Carved plinth base.

Height, 30½ inches; length, 55 inches

359. GEORGIAN CARVED MAHOGANY BOW-FRONT CORNER CUPBOARD
Glazed latticed doors surmounted by a pierced and carved swanneck pediment; the lower part with one long drawer over a double paneled cupboard. Bracket feet. *Height, 6 feet 6 inches; width, 31 inches*

[NUMBER 360]

360. CARVED MAHOGANY BREAK-FRONT SECRETARY BOOKCASE

Recessed upper part with four latticed glazed doors enclosing adjustable shelves, surmounted by dentiled cornice with pierced and molded swanneck pediment; lower part fitted with two short drawers and secretary drawer with fitted interior, above four paneled cupboard doors. Molded base, bracket feet.　　　　*Height, 7 feet 2 inches; width, 5 feet 1 inch*

[See illustration]

53

361. **PAIR CARVED MAHOGANY TALL-POST BEDSTEADS**

Single bedsteads in the Samuel McIntire taste; the head and foot posts slender reeded columns with carved swags and leafage. Quadrangular legs and spade feet; scrolled and shaped headboards.

Height, 5 feet 10 inches; length, 6 feet 6 inches; width, 39 inches

362. **CARVED MAHOGANY TRIPOD STAND** *Chippendale Style*

Top with piecrust ribbon-carved edge on fluted shaft and acanthus-carved claw-and-ball-footed cabriole legs.

Height, 21 inches; diameter, 15 inches

363. **GEORGIAN INLAID MAHOGANY PEMBROKE TABLE**

Slightly bowed central section with two cyma-shaped drop leaves, frieze containing one drawer; square tapering legs, plinth feet.

Height, 29½ inches; length open, 42 inches

364. **MAPLE AND CURLY MAPLE SLANT-LID DESK**

American, XVIII Century

With stepped fitted interior, four drawers of graduated depth, shaped valance, and bracket feet; willow brasses. Refinished.

Height, 42½ inches; length, 37 inches

365. **QUEEN ANNE FIGURED WALNUT LOWBOY**

With cove-molded top, three drawers with solid-back brasses, triple-arched skirt, and cabriole legs terminating in web feet.

Height, 28¾ inches; length, 35½ inches

366. **PIERCED BRASS FENDER** *English, Early XIX Century*

Molded top banded with double row of pierced leafage; paw feet.

Length, 41 inches

367. **PAIR BRASS ANDIRONS AND FOUR FIRE TOOLS** *Early XIX Century*

Ring-turned andirons with spurred supports, ball feet. Fire tools consisting of shovel and three tongs. *Height of andirons, 17 inches*

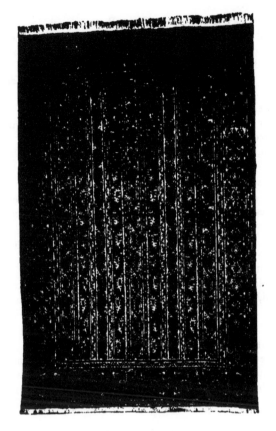

[NU‸BER 368]

TRANSCASPIAN RUGS [CONCLUDED]

68. TRANSCASPIAN RUG

So-called border rug with unusual design of stripes, each with cloud bands and flame motives; in violet, blue, yellow, and cream. Worn. Interesting because of the variety of geometrical and ornamental borders.

Length, 8 feet 3 inches; width, 5 feet 2 inches

[See illustration]

69. YON UD-HATSCHLU RUG

Allover floral and ornamental decoration in four sections, in red, blue, brown, and white; different floral and geometrical borders, ornamental ends.   *Length, 5 feet 3 inches; width, 4 feet 1 inch*

70. TWO BALUCHISTAN PRAYER RUGS

One with long tree in foliage surrounded by floral forms in dark red, blue, violet, and white on a mocha ground; nine geometric and floral borders. The other slightly different, with ten borders.

Length, 5 feet 4 inches; width, 2 feet 9 inches
Length, 4 feet 10 inches; width, 2 feet 9 inches

371. PAIR TEKKE TURKOMAN TENT BAGS

Shaped oval emblems and ornamental diamond forms in red, blue, and cream on a red ground; three floral and geometrical borders and one leaf garland border on the top.

Length, 3 feet 9 inches; width, 2 feet 5 inches

372. PENDEH RUG

Prayer design in four sections, with geometrical pattern in dark blue on a rich red field; different geometrical and floral borders in blue, white, and brown, one floral end. *Length, 5 feet 4 inches; width, 4 feet 2 inches*

373. TRANSCASPIAN RUG

Large multicolored stylized 'pear' forms on cream ground with scattered rosettes, symbolical and geometrical forms; in seven geometrical and floral borders in red, green, blue, yellow, and cream.

Length, 6 feet 3 inches; width, 4 feet 7 inches

374. YONUD BOKHARA RUG

Unusual design of diamond lattice centring latchhooked geometrical signs in red, blue, and white; seven geometrical and ornamental borders, floral ends. *Length, 6 feet; width, 3 feet 9 inches*

375. BESHIR RUG

Allover design of blossoming branches and rosettes and animal forms in an unusual arrangement on a rich red field; in yellow, green, cream, and dark blue; eleven geometrical and floral borders. Very thick pile.

Length, 5 feet 4 inches; width, 4 feet 5 inches

376. TURKOMAN RUG WITH KAZAK DESIGN

Elongated geometrical medallion surrounded by trees, in rose, blue, white, yellow, green, and brown; leaf-and-wine-cup and five other geometrical borders. *Length, 6 feet; width, 3 feet 8 inches*

377. YONUD BOKHARA RUG

Rows of oval shaped medallions in white, blue, red, and orange; on a red plum field; three floral and geometrical borders, floral ends.

Length, 4 feet 4 inches; width, 3 feet

378. SEREBEND RUG

Tile red ground with allover pattern of multicolored pears; eight geometrical borders in green, blue, cream, and red.

Length, 6 feet 9 inches; width, 4 feet 4 inches

379. YONUD-HATSCHLU RUG

Floral decoration, in four sections, on violet brown ground, in red, blue, green, and white. Four geometrical, ornamental, and floral borders; two ornamental ends. *Length, 5 feet 10 inches; width, 4 feet 1 inch*

[NUMBER 380]

380. SHIRAZ RUG

In the taste of the Herati Beshir, with rows of large stylized 'pear' forms having floral and animal decoration on cream field in wine red, tile red, blue, yellow, brown, and green; seven geometrical and floral borders, two geometrical ends.　*Length, 6 feet 2 inches; width, 4 feet 5 inches*

[See illustration]

381. TEKKE TURKOMAN RUG

Rows of ornamental oval emblems in red, brown, dark blue, and cream on a red-brown ground; seven floral and geometrical borders, two geometrical ends. Worn.　*Length, 5 feet 6 inches; width, 4 feet*

382. YOMUD BOKHARA RUG

Rows of shaped oval medallions in orange, dark blue, red, and white on a brown-red ground; geometric and floral borders, ornamental ends.
Length, 4 feet 4 inches; width, 2 feet 11 inches

57

383. YONUD-HATSCHLU RUG

Floral decoration, in four sections, on wine red ground, in green, blue, orange, and white; five floral and geometrical borders, two ornamental ends. *Length, 5 feet 9 inches; width, 4 feet 2 inches*

384. BALUCHISTAN RUG

Long central panel with 'tree of life' motive in dark red, brown, white, and blue on *café au lait* ground; eight floral, geometrical, lace, and rosette borders. . *Length, 5 feet 1 inch; width, 2 feet 8 inches*

385. AFGHAN RUNNER

Rows of linked octagonal medallions; six ornamental and floral borders in tile red, green, and blue on red-brown ground. *Length, 7 feet 6 inches; width, 3 feet 4 inches.*

386. BALUCHISTAN RUG

Geometrical shaped medallion ornamented with geometrical and floral decoration; different geometrical and ornamental borders, all on red-brown ground, in violet, white, blue, and salmon. *Length, 5 feet; width, 3 feet 7 inches*

387. BESHIR RUG

Floral ornamental medallions on a plum-colored field, with geometric signs in red, yellow, blue, and white; four geometrical borders. *Length, 5 feet 3 inches; width, 3 feet 2 inches*

388. AFGHAN RUG

Deep terra cotta field with floral octagons and symbolical signs; four floral and geometrical borders, in blue, green, and tile red. Worn. *Length, 5 feet 4 inches; width, 3 feet 11 inches*

389. TEKKE TURKONAN RUG

Rows of oval medallions interspersed with diamond forms, on wine red ground, in blue, cream, and tile red; five geometrical and floral borders, two different geometrical ends. *Length, 4 feet 2 inches; width, 3 feet 4 inches*

390. BALUCHISTAN RUG

Centre panel with rectangles, each containing an ornamental medallion, in dark blue, white, and brown on bright red ground; seven floral and geometrical borders. *Length, 5 feet 8 inches; width, 2 feet 6 inches*

391. KAZAK RUG

With unusual prayer design, dark blue mihrab with two cross-shaped medallions, one tile red, the other green; with yellow and light blue floral decorations in wine red. Seven geometrical and floral borders; signed. *Length, 4 feet 10 inches; width, 2 feet 7 inches*

. AFGHAN RUG
Two rows of connected octagons, with trefoil decoration, in brown and deep blue on red ground; three floral and ornamental borders. Slightly worn.
Length, 4 feet 9 inches; width, 3 feet 3 inches

. BALUCHISTAN PRAYER RUG
Blossoming 'tree of life' on mocha ground; three geometrical borders in rich dark red, blue, and white. Two small matching rectangles in corners. In brown, red, and dark blue.
Length, 4 feet 2 inches; width, 2 feet 7 inches

TEXTILES

. IVORY-EMBROIDERED MAUVE SATIN COVERLET
Embroidered in ecru silks with graceful sprays of blossoms. Lined and interlined.
Length, 8 feet 8 inches; width, 7 feet 7 inches

. TWO CHASUBLES
One in green silk and silver brocade with orphreys of flowered ivory brocade; the other of embroidered deep peach satin, damaged.

. GOLD-EMBROIDERED GREEN SILK ALTAR FRONTAL
Finely embroidered with the story of the dragon in pursuit of the sacred jewel; fringed.
Length, 9 feet 1 inch; width, 17 inches

. TWO NEEDLEPOINT CUSHIONS
Fringed.

. THREE ASSORTED TEXTILE PANELS

. TWO CRIMSON VELVET CUSHIONS
One with silver embroidery in the design of the Sacred Heart, the other with appliqué panel of silk needlepoint. Both fringed.

Photographs by
Lawrence X. Champeau

Half-tone Plates by
Walker Engraving Corporation
Composition and Presswork
by

PUBLISHERS PRINTING COMPANY
William Bradford Press
NEW YORK